Current
CONTROVERSIES

Violence Against Women

Other books in the Current Controversies series

CONTROVERSIES

DISCARD

Violence Against Women

Kate Burns, Book Editor

GREENHAVEN PRESS
An imprint of Thomson Gale, a part of The Thomson Corporation

THOMSON

GALE

Detroit • New York • San Francisco • New Haven, Conn. • Waterville, Maine • London

362.88082
V795
2008

Christine Nasso, *Publisher*
Elizabeth Des Chenes, *Managing Editor*

© 2008 The Gale Group.

Star logo is a trademark and Gale and Greenhaven Press are registered trademarks used herein under license.

For more information, contact:
Greenhaven Press
27500 Drake Rd.
Farmington Hills, MI 48331-3535
Or you can visit our Internet site at http://www.gale.com

LIBRARY OF CONGRESS CATALOGING-IN-PUBLICATION DATA

Violence Against Women / Kate Burns, Editor.
    p. cm. -- (Current controversies)
    Includes bibliographical references and index.
    ISBN-13: 978-0-7377-3729-5 (hardcover)
    ISBN-13: 978-0-7377-3730-1 (pbk.)
    1. Women--Violence against--United States. I. Burns, Kate, 1963-
    HV6250.4.W65V52233 2008
    362.88082'0973--dc22

                                                2007029806

ISBN-10: 0-7377-3729-8 (hardcover)
ISBN-10: 0-7377-3730-1 (pbk.)

Printed in the United States of America
10 9 8 7 6 5 4 3 2 1

Contents

No: The Problem of Violence in the United States Has Been Misrepresented

Chapter 2: What Causes Violence Against Women?

Chapter 3: Are Current Approaches to Reducing Violence Against Women Effective?

Foreword

By definition, controversies are "discussions of questions in which opposing opinions clash" (Webster's Twentieth Century Dictionary Unabridged). Few would deny that controversies are a pervasive part of the human condition and exist on virtually every level of human enterprise. Controversies transpire between individuals and among groups, within nations and between nations. Controversies supply the grist necessary for progress by providing challenges and challengers to the status quo. They also create atmospheres where strife and warfare can flourish. A world without controversies would be a peaceful world; but it also would be, by and large, static and prosaic.

The Series' Purpose

The purpose of the Current Controversies series is to explore many of the social, political, and economic controversies dominating the national and international scenes today. Titles selected for inclusion in the series are highly focused and specific. For example, from the larger category of criminal justice, Current Controversies deals with specific topics such as police brutality, gun control, white collar crime, and others. The debates in Current Controversies also are presented in a useful, timeless fashion. Articles and book excerpts included in each title are selected if they contribute valuable, long-range ideas to the overall debate. And wherever possible, current information is enhanced with historical documents and other relevant materials. Thus, while individual titles are current in focus, every effort is made to ensure that they will not become quickly outdated. Books in the Current Controversies series will remain important resources for librarians, teachers, and students for many years.

In addition to keeping the titles focused and specific, great care is taken in the editorial format of each book in the series. Book introductions and chapter prefaces are offered to provide background material for readers. Chapters are organized around several key questions that are answered with diverse opinions representing all points on the political spectrum. Materials in each chapter include opinions in which authors clearly disagree as well as alternative opinions in which authors may agree on a broader issue but disagree on the possible solutions. In this way, the content of each volume in Current Controversies mirrors the mosaic of opinions encountered in society. Readers will quickly realize that there are many viable answers to these complex issues. By questioning each author's conclusions, students and casual readers can begin to develop the critical thinking skills so important to evaluating opinionated material.

Current Controversies is also ideal for controlled research. Each anthology in the series is composed of primary sources taken from a wide gamut of informational categories including periodicals, newspapers, books, U.S. and foreign government documents, and the publications of private and public organizations. Readers will find factual support for reports, debates, and research papers covering all areas of important issues. In addition, an annotated table of contents, an index, a book and periodical bibliography, and a list of organizations to contact are included in each book to expedite further research.

Perhaps more than ever before in history, people are confronted with diverse and contradictory information. During the Persian Gulf War, for example, the public was not only treated to minute-to-minute coverage of the war, it was also inundated with critiques of the coverage and countless analyses of the factors motivating U.S. involvement. Being able to sort through the plethora of opinions accompanying today's major issues, and to draw one's own conclusions, can be a complicated and frustrating struggle. It is the editors' hope that Current Controversies will help readers with this struggle.

Introduction

"Deeply held preconceptions about gender perpetuate the notion that violent behavior is the exclusive territory of boys and men."

Three teenagers ambush a twelve-year-old girl just outside her elementary school in Suffolk County, New York. They savagely pull her by the hair until she is knocked down and then repeatedly hit and kick her in the face and body. Adding insult to injury, the three bullies recruit a friend to videotape the incident as it is happening. Shortly after the December 18, 2006, beating, they post the video on YouTube, a video-sharing Web site where users can upload their homemade videos for public viewing. Soon hundreds of students in the area are watching the recorded event on their computers and mobile Internet devices. When the media discovers the sensational story, news programs across the country replay the YouTube video for television viewers. As word gets out, thousands more from around the globe log on to YouTube to see the shocking scene for themselves.

Predictably, this notorious YouTube video prompted much public debate about the ethical implications of posting violent home movies on video-sharing Web sites. It also generated anxious discussions on the topic of violence against women. Many viewers were shocked by the identity of the attackers—all of whom were female. The video graphically documented a problem that has become a growing concern for girls, their parents and teachers, and child psychologists: the rise in girl-on-girl violence. Crime statistics seem to support the fact that girls are becoming more violent. The U.S. Justice Department's Uniform Crime Report shows that from 1992 to 2003, the number of girls arrested nationwide for assault rose 41 percent, as opposed to a mere 4.3 increase among boys. Statistics aside, seeing three girls so brutally beat another girl shattered an assumption held by many—that bullying is primarily a problem of boy-on-boy aggression. Deeply held preconceptions about gender perpetuate the notion that violent behavior is the exclusive territory of boys and men.

This assumption is also prevalent in research about violence against women. Moreover, most domestic violence recovery programs base their treatment on the premise that men perpetrate violence because sexism and male privilege lead them to undervalue and even despise women. While that premise may be accurate in many instances, it may not be useful in the healing process of both victims and perpetrators of female-on-female violence. There is clear evidence that women commit *some* of the violence against women, though certainly not the majority of it. Some say that female-on-female violence happens enough to adjust dominant theories about causes and prevention of violence against women. They argue that it also justifies altering recovery programs for victims and perpetrators. In addition to girl-on-girl bullying, two other types of female-on-female violence in particular make this question worth considering: domestic violence and sexual assault.

Female-on-female domestic violence has been shown to exist in several types of relationships, including mother-on-daughter child abuse, daughter-on-mother elder abuse, and intimate abuse in lesbian couples. Perhaps the most comparable to domestic violence in heterosexual couples, lesbian battering was a taboo subject in the field of domestic violence prevention for many years. The reasons for the silence surrounding lesbian battering are varied and complex, but in the last decade some in the field have begun to assert that avoiding the topic only makes the situation much worse for victims. The scarcity of research about the problem makes it difficult to determine the actual number of lesbians who are battered each year, but many workers in the battered women's movement estimate that it takes place approximately as often as domestic violence occurs in heterosexual relationships.

Psychologist Ellyn Kaschak says that taking lesbian battering into account may rattle the foundations of current policy and practices developed to combat domestic violence. She writes in her book *Intimate Betrayal: Domestic Violence in Lesbian Relationships*:

> The existence of violence in lesbian relationships calls into question some of the most accepted explanations for intimate violence and highlights the necessity for developing models of intervention that are appropriate and effective in the circumstance of a relationship between women, ones that take into consideration both the similarities to and differences from violence in intimate heterosexual and in gay male relationships.

Her comments suggest some questions to keep in mind while exploring this book. How do assumptions about gender shape understanding about what causes domestic violence? Do sexism and misogyny underlie the actions of female perpetrators of violence against women? What other models might also explain female-on-female violence?

While it is common to associate physical violence with male gender roles, it is even more customary to link sexual violence with masculinity. Yet, girls and women have been sexually assaulted by women. Recently, there has been more discussion of women as possible perpetrators of child sexual abuse in psychological literature. There is still disagreement about just how frequently women sexually abuse children, and especially female children. Professor of social work Renee Koonin notes that child psychologists have only recently won the battle to place gender and male power at the center of an analysis of sexual abuse; therefore, they are reluctant to focus attention on female abusers. However, she writes, "a significant minority of victims are abused by women and it is essential that no child should be silenced by ideology which denies the reality of abuse by females."

If female-perpetrated child sexual abuse is hard to acknowledge, female-on-female rape occurring between adults may be extremely difficult for many to believe. Part of the problem is that researchers reinforce the idea that women do not perpetrate sexual assault. For example, the Centers for Disease Control and Prevention states on their 2007 *Sexual Violence: Fact Sheet* that "100% of rapes . . . were perpetrated by men." Nevertheless, enough women have come forward with evidence of being sexually assaulted by other women that a few antiviolence programs have started collecting statistics and addressing the problem. Writing for the lesbian magazine *Curve*, Jane Lowers reports that "studies show that as many as a third of lesbians have been victims of sexual assault or coercion at the hands of another woman." Definitions of woman-on-woman rape include unwanted or violent penetration, forcing the victim to perform a sexual act, or any form of nonconsensual sex forced on the victim.

Does the fact that female-on-female violence exists require new theories to explain violence against women? Researchers like Charles E. Corry, Martin S. Fiebert, and Erin Pizzey believe that the dominant theory, which argues that sexism and male power lead to violence against women, needs to be abandoned. In their book, *Controlling Domestic Violence Against Men*, they assert that domestic violence and abuse should be seen as human issues, not as gender issues. However, Lori B. Girshick, author of *Woman to Woman Sexual Violence: Does She Call It Rape?* disagrees. Rather than discard groundbreaking feminist insights about violence, she instead recommends acknowledging power differentials in addition to gender that may also exist between women. She writes:

> That same-sex abuse between women does exist does not mean we have to throw out our feminist analysis about rape and battering. However, using a framework where male

privilege is just one aspect of the broader hierarchical power-over model is more useful. This model allows us to be more inclusive of the interrelated issues of race, class, age, and ability, as well as sex, in terms of power and control dynamics and abuse.

In her analysis, violence can result when a conflicted relationship is characterized by a marked power imbalance. Girshick's approach still recognizes that women *in general* are not equal to men in many ways. It also accounts for the fact that inequalities exist among women, and therefore can lead to violence against other women if combined with other mitigating factors.

Female-on-female violence is just one of the controversial issues surrounding the complex problem of violence against women. The essays included in this volume highlight heated debates about the prevalence of, the causes of, and the remedies for violence against women. *Current Controversies: Violence Against Women* offers a wealth of material to explore a disturbing and multifaceted problem.

CHAPTER 1

Is Violence Against Women in the United States a Serious Problem?

Chapter Preface

An examination of the prevalence of violence against women in the United States is incomplete without considering the situation of indigenous American women. For the National Organization of Women, Lisa Bhungalia writes that "Native American women experience the highest rate of violence of any group in the United States." A Department of Justice report, *American Indians and Crime*, states that Native American women suffer violent crime three and a half times more often than the national average. According to other researchers, this number is actually much higher because over 70 percent of sexual assaults go unreported.

Why are Native American women subjected to so much violence? Many researchers cite the long history of colonial racism as a mitigating factor. Andrea Smith notes that throughout the eighteenth and nineteenth centuries, Anglo-European settlers viewed the subjugation of indigenous women as a sign of the success of economic, cultural, and political colonization. In contrast to the patriarchal order of Anglo-European culture, Native societies were relatively more egalitarian and peaceful. The high status of Native women unsettled the European social order that viewed women and children as the property of men. In her essay "Not an Indian Tradition: The Sexual Colonization of Native Peoples," Smith writes that "Native women as bearers of a counter-imperial order pose[d] a supreme threat to the imperial order. Symbolic and literal control over their bodies [was] important in the war against Native people." While white women were venerated as the pure and clean bearers of civilization, indigenous women were categorized as unclean and therefore sexually violable. "The rape of bodies that are considered inherently impure or dirty simply does not count," explains Smith.

Yet does the colonial tradition of the distant past explain why Native American women are victimized more in the present? Victim advocates note two reasons why it does. First, the colonial desire to conquer Indian women's bodies is still a titillating temptation for the masculine Anglo-American imagination. For example, Stuart Kasten capitalized on it when he designed his video game called "Custer's Revenge" in 1982. In the game, players get points each time they rape an Indian woman. The promotional material promises:

> You are the General Custer. Your dander's up, your pistol's wavin'. You've hog-tied a ravishing Indian maiden and have a chance to rewrite history and even up an old score. Now, the Indian maiden's hands may be tied, but she's not about to take it lying down, by George! Help is on the way. If you're to get revenge you'll have to rise to the challenge, dodge a tribe of flying arrows and protect your flanks against some downright mean and prickly cactus. But if you can stand pat and last past the strings and arrows—You can stand last. Remember? Revenge is sweet.

Some may argue that images like these in popular culture do not necessarily reflect reality. Yet federal surveys show again and again that the majority of violence against Indian women involves non-Indian perpetrators.

If the cultural prevalence of derogatory images and stereotypes about Native American women is not enough to explain the violence they face, then perhaps the lack of concern or retribution in the legal system does. The second colonial inheritance that victim advocates frequently cite as part of the problem facing Native American women is the faulty justice system. A pamphlet by the National Sexual Violence Resource Center describes the governance of Indian country as "a jurisdictional maze." Federal prosecutors frequently decline to prosecute crimes involving Indian territory, deferring instead to tribal jurisdiction. Meanwhile, tribal police agencies and courts are severely understaffed and unable to adequately deal with the scope of the problem. Further aggravating the issue of racial inequality, tribal courts essentially have no jurisdiction over non-Indian perpetrators. The non-Indian men who are most likely to perpetrate violence against Indian women are also more likely to escape punishment for their crimes. These and other factors place Native American women at significant risk for domestic violence and sexual abuse. Most do not seek justice because they know they will be met with inaction or indifference.

Domestic violence and sexual assault are devastating for all women in the United States. However, when it is allowed to go unpunished, it compounds the violation for the victim. Authors in the following chapter debate the seriousness of violence against women for several different groups in the United States.

Violence Against Women in the United States Is a Serious Problem

Brittney Nichols

Brittney Nichols is pursuing her master's degree in clinical psychology at the University of Texas at Tyler and is an advocate for the East Texas Crisis Center where she received a HOPE award for her work in 2005.

Violence against women is one of the most prevalent problems in America. The men who are committing these violent acts are not strangers to their victims. When women are attacked, it is most often by men they know. In 2004, men were as likely to be victimized by a stranger as by someone they knew, but women were most often victimized by someone they knew.

Nicole Brown Simpson

The murder trial of Nicole Brown Simpson captivated the nation [in 1995]. The celebrity status of [former football star] O.J. Simpson and race issues dominated public discussion, overshadowing the core issue of the case, which was domestic violence. The evidence presented at the trial included a history of domestic abuse, something O.J. didn't deny. During the investigation, it came to light that Nicole rented a safe-deposit box. The box contained a picture of Nicole with a black eye. It also held letters containing apologies from O.J. to Nicole for abusing her; in one letter, O.J. acknowledged the fact that he abused Nicole because she refused to have sex with him. The prosecution tried to focus on domestic violence as being important to the case, but the brutal beatings that Nicole endured at the hands of O.J. were largely dismissed, even though it is common for domestic violence to escalate to homicide. A former cop and friend of O.J. testified that, at Nicole's request, he had warned O.J. that he fit the pattern of an abuser. Despite evidence to the contrary, one of defense lawyer Johnnie Cochran's arguments at trial was that not every man who beats his wife murders her. Five days before Nicole was brutally murdered, she phoned a shelter and was frightened that O.J. was going to kill her. Domestic abuse advocates understand how domestic abuse and violence often escalate to murder, but this fact did not appear to be taken seriously at the trial. A juror called a 911 tape recording of Nicole begging for help as O.J. shouted at her "a waste of time." O.J. Simpson was acquitted October 3, 1995.

The more the abusers feel the lack of control, the more they will act to regain it.

Other High Profile Cases

The disappearance of Laci Peterson caught the nation's attention in 2003. Laci was reported missing on December 24, 2002. Her body and that of her unborn son (already named Connor) washed up on the California shore in April 2003. Although Laci's husband, Scott, was a suspect, Laci's family supported him in the early days of the investigation, describing him as a "loving husband" and "model son-in-law." He was eventually convicted of killing his wife and dumping her body in the San Francisco Bay. If Amber Frey, the woman with whom Scott was having an affair a month before Laci's disappearance, had not come forward, he might have gotten away with the murder. Amber helped the police catch Scott in several lies by cooperating with the investigation and taping his phone calls to her.

Mark Hacking admitted to a Salt Lake City judge, "I intentionally shot Lori Hacking in the head with a .22 rifle on July 19, 2004." After killing Lori, Mark had reported her missing, saying that she had not returned from a jog. Lori had recently discovered she was pregnant, and the couple had planned a move to North Carolina for Mark to attend medical school. They had found an apartment, arranged for a moving truck, and packed. However, during the search for her body, it was discovered that Mark had been living a lie. Investigators learned that Mark had not been admitted to medical school (he never even applied); he also had not graduated from college. Mark killed his wife after she discovered his secret.

David Brame was a police chief. The city of Tacoma was shocked in April 2003, when he shot his wife before turning the gun on himself. What at first appeared to be a random act of violence was actually preceded by a history of domestic abuse. Crystal Brame had filed for divorce in February before the shooting. It was then that she spoke up about her husband's violence, revealing that he had choked her four times the year before, shoved her in a closet, and pointed a gun at her head. She also divulged to her psychologist that David was pressuring her to participate in group sex. David kept Crystal in an intimidating environment not only through physical violence but also by playing mind games and making threats. David called her mentally unstable and threatened to take away her children (a son and a daughter), if she left. Given David's position in the community, Crystal felt she had no one to turn to for help.

Obsession with Control

Although these cases appear to be isolated tragedies, they have consistent themes. One major theme is that of control. Many abusers feel a strong need to control the behavior of their partner. The threat of a breakup or divorce threatens that sense of control, while their need for it escalates. When abusers feel that they are losing control, they increase the violence and intimidation. Nicole and O.J. were divorced in 1992. In the time leading up to her murder [in June 1994], friends and family reported that Nicole was reducing her contact with O.J. and disengaging from her relationship with him. Instead of letting go, O.J. stalked Nicole by following her and peeking into her windows.

Perhaps the most horrendous thing about these crimes is that they and the people who commit them are not unique or unusual.

Crystal Brame described her husband's controlling behavior in court papers. His behavior included making her get permission to use their credit card and monitoring her trips to the grocery store by checking the car's odometer. Leaving an abusive partner often triggers more controlling behavior, more abuse, and, all too often, murder.

Manipulation

Another common theme is manipulation. Like Scott Peterson and Mark Hacking, abusers often spin a web of lies to cover their tracks and even blame the victims for their behavior. Ironically, they are often well liked and popular, even charming—a trait that comes in handy when they need to hide the truth of what they are really like. A childhood friend of David Brame said that David never appeared to be a violent person. In fact, the friend described him as a "class act." To continue his affair, Scott Peterson lied to Amber Frey about several things, including his marital status. He also told Amber on the phone that he was celebrating New Year's Eve 2003 in Paris, when he was actually at a candlelight vigil for his missing wife in Modesto, California. The lies told by these men gave them a temporary sense of control, but when the lies started to fall apart, their control quickly began to slip away. Like many abusers, these men were apparently so unable to deal with the loss of control they were willing to go to extreme lengths to regain control, even if it meant murder. Mark Hacking managed to convince everyone he knew that he was living a different life. He went to extremes to support the fantasy, such as picking out an apartment near the medical school he was never going to attend. When his wife discovered his secret, he panicked and killed her to protect the secrets of his false life. In general, the more the abusers feel the lack of control, the more they will act to regain it. Men often try to regain control with intimidation and violence, and all too often this has deadly consequences. . . .

Who Is that Guy Next Door?

On the surface, the men who commit these crimes do not appear to be cold-blooded killers or psychotic maniacs. Many are accomplished role models or the guy next door. They are our neighbors. They are seemingly upstanding citizens, from all walks of life. These cases, as shocking as they are, are not that unusual. We may want to believe that these crimes are committed under rare or unusual circumstances by people who are psychotic or monstrous, but it is not so. Perhaps the most horrendous thing about these crimes is that they and the people who commit them are not unique or unusual. Our society has not yet widely acknowledged how common these crimes are and what a challenge it is to address the circumstances that lead to such occurrences.

When women are sexually assaulted, it is most likely to be by a friend or acquaintance.

These stories are tragic. However, they help to bring attention to the rampant problem of violence against women in this country. This can provide a gateway for discussion, instill awareness, and help to spawn change. The diversity of the victims in these stories shows that abuse can happen to anyone. Victims of abuse should not feel stigmatized or alone in their experiences. It is hoped that these tragedies will encourage women suffering physical or emotional abuse to get help before their situation turns deadly. During the Simpson trial, as women realized that what had happened to Nicole could happen to them, domestic violence calls increased.

Physical Abuse

Physical abuse includes slapping, hitting, kicking, burning, punching, choking, shoving, beating, throwing things, locking a person out of the house, restraining, and other acts designed to injure, hurt, endanger, or cause physical pain.

By the most conservative estimates, one million women in the United States suffer nonfatal violence by a spouse or partner each year. In 2001, more than half a million American women (588,490) reported being victims of nonfatal violence committed by an intimate partner; undoubtedly, many other cases went unreported. Physical abuse is such a common problem that it is very likely that someone you know has experienced it or is currently in an abusive relationship. Thirty percent of Americans say they know a woman who has been physically abused by her husband or boyfriend in the past year. Although these statistics are staggering, they only give part of the picture. Many acts of violence go unreported and are hidden even from friends and family.

The following vignettes are examples of physical abuse:

Sarah is cooking dinner when her husband, Matt, comes home from work. He is angry that the meal isn't ready and begins to complain. He calls her incompetent and throws a pot of boiling water at her, causing serious burns.

Jennifer breaks up with her boyfriend Nick and begins dating another guy. Jealous, Nick follows her home one night and attacks her before she is safely inside. He kicks and punches her, calls her a slut, and leaves her with several bruises and a broken jaw.

Sharon's husband, Ted, is screaming at their five-year-old daughter for leaving a mess on the floor. Sharon suggests that he calm down. He then slaps Sharon, shouting that the house is his house and he can scream all he wants.

Sexual Abuse

Sexual abuse includes sadism and forcing a person to have sex when he or she does not want to; forcing a person to engage in sexual acts that he or she does not like or finds unpleasant, frightening, or violent; forcing a person to have sex with others or while others watch; or forcing a person into acts that make him or her feel sexually demeaned or violated. Sexual abuse may also include forcing a woman into reproductive decisions that are contrary to her wishes or forcing her to have sex without protection against disease or pregnancy.

When we think of rape in America, the typical scenario we imagine is a young woman being attacked in a dark alley by a stranger. Although rape is certainly perpetrated by strangers, this common stereotype of the crime does not convey the whole story or even the most common story. When women are sexually assaulted, it is most likely to be by a friend or acquaintance. In their lifetime, one in four women are likely to experience sexual violence by an intimate partner. In 2001, 41,470 women reported rape/sexual assault committed by an intimate partner. However, these numbers only give us a fraction of the picture, because rape is the most underreported violent crime in the country. Victims often know their attacker. In a survey of victims who did not report either rape or attempted rape to the police, they stated the following reasons why no report was made: 43 percent thought nothing could be done, 27 percent felt it was a private matter, 12 percent were afraid of police response, and 12 percent felt it would not be seen as that important.

All of the following vignettes are examples of sexual abuse:

Jeff secretly videotapes his girlfriend Shannon having sex with him. He then shows the tape to a group of his friends, knowing that Shannon would never have consented to such an act.

John forces his wife, Mary, to have sex when she doesn't want to do so. He laughs afterward, calling her a prude, and tells her that it is his right as her husband.

Bryan and Cindy have five children. Cindy is overwhelmed, and they have agreed not to have any more children. To keep Cindy busy at home, Bryan tampers with her birth control and she becomes pregnant.

Financially speaking, the cost of domestic violence is tremendous.

Emotional Abuse

Emotional abuse includes consistently doing or saying things to shame, insult, ridicule, embarrass, demean, belittle, or mentally hurt another person. This may include calling a person names such as fat, lazy, stupid, bitch, silly, ugly, or failure, or telling someone he or she can't do anything right, is worthless, is undeserving, or is unwanted. Emotional abuse may also involve withholding money, affection, attention, or permission; destroying property; forcing a person to do things he or she does not want to do; manipulating; hurting or threatening children or pets; threatening to either abandon a person or take his or her children away. It may also include refusing to help someone who is sick or hurt; ridiculing a person's valued beliefs, religion, race, heritage, or class; or insulting a person's family or friends.

Emotional abuse is less recognized as a significant social problem, but it is very harmful, quite common, and often occurs in conjunction with physical and sexual abuse. Due to the nature of emotional abuse, it is difficult to get accurate information on its prevalence. Some studies estimate that emotional abuse is 22 percent more prevalent than physical abuse. Many people mistakenly believe that if there has been no physical damage, the behavior is not abusive and does not cause real harm. Ironically, emotional abuse is often described by victims as being worse than the physical abuse. The scars it leaves remain long after physical bruises have healed.

Here are examples of emotional abuse:

While Debbie fixes her hair in the morning, her live-in boyfriend, Tim, belittles her. He calls her names and tells her that she is wasting her time trying to look nice, because she will always be ugly.

Rob constantly comes home and complains that his wife, Sandra, is ruining his life. He tells her that he knows that he can find someone better and that someday he is going to take the children and leave.

Clearly, intimate violence against women has a profound impact on many facets of our society. It affects women of every age, race, or social status. Globally, one in three women has been beaten, coerced into sex, or otherwise abused in her lifetime. According to the American Medical Association, family violence kills as many women every five years as the total number of Americans who died in the Vietnam War. Financially speaking, the cost of domestic violence is tremendous. According to a study by the Centers for Disease Control and Prevention (CDC), the health-related costs of rape, physical assault, stalking, and homicide by intimate partners exceed $5.8 billion each year, including $4.1 billion in direct health care expenses, $900 million in lost productivity, and $900 million in lifetime earnings. Businesses lose about $100 million annually in lost wages, sick leave, absenteeism, and nonproductivity as a direct result of domestic violence. . . .

These statistics show that despite the tendency in our country to dismiss violence between intimate partners as a private matter, the damage it causes reaches far beyond the closed doors it hides behind. The numbers clearly show that this is not an individual problem—this is society's problem. It is time to bring attention to this matter and ask ourselves why, in a country that glorifies rights and freedoms, we fail to deliver to women the right to live without fear of violence. Despite being the richest country in the world, the United States has some of the highest rates for rape, domestic violence, and spousal murder. Rape, for instance, is 18 times higher in the United States than in Great Britain, and rape is one of the few categories of crime in the United States that has not seen a decrease in recent years. Such numbers tell us that we are still too tolerant of violence directed at women. As a culture, we continue to believe that violence against women is a "normal" interaction between men and women. It is time that we find such behavior completely unacceptable.

Rape Is a Serious Problem for Women

Office for Victims of Crime

The Office for Victims of Crime is a bureau of the U.S. Department of Justice established by the 1984 Victims of Crime Act to oversee diverse programs that benefit victims of crime.

According to the [2004] National Crime Victimization Survey [by the U.S. Department of Justice] there were 198,850 rapes and sexual assaults measured in 2003.

Among female victims of rape and sexual assault, 70 percent of the crimes were committed by intimates, other relatives, friends or acquaintances.

According to the National Crime Victimization Survey, the average number of rapes and sexual assaults during 2002 and 2003 was 223,290 of which 81,310 crimes were rapes; 61,060 were attempted rapes, and 80,910 were sexual assaults.

In 2003, weapons were present in rapes and sexual assaults 11 percent of the time.

The annual rate of rapes and sexual assaults overall between 1993 and 2003 declined 68 percent.

In 2003, 38.5 percent of rapes and sexual assaults were reported to the police.

[According to the U.S. Department of Defense,] in 2002 and 2003 respectively, 69.1 and 70.0 alleged sexual assaults were reported per 100,000 uniformed service members. Across the Department of Defense, there were 901 cases reported of uniformed service victims in 2002 and 1,012 cases reported in 2003.

Office for Victims of Crime, "Rape and Sexual Assault," *2006 Resource Guide for National Crime Victims' Rights Week*. U.S. Department of Justice, 2006. http://www.ojp.usdoj.gov/ovc/ncvrw/2006/pdf/statistical_overviews.pdf

Juvenile Offenders and Victims

[The U.S. Department of Justice reported in 2004 that] victims of sexual assault committed by juveniles are younger than 18 years of age approximately 96 percent of the time.

There were 95,136 forcible rapes of females in 2002, representing a 4.7 increase from the previous year.

Adult victims of juvenile sex offenders were much less likely to be strangers than were adult victims of adult sex offenders.

More than one in four victims of a juvenile or adult sex offender was a family member.

Sexual Assault in Small Communities

Contrary to common belief that violent crime rates are notably lower in rural areas, a recent analysis of location data collected for the 1989 National Women's Study found that 10.1 percent of women living in rural areas had experienced a completed rape compared to 13.6 percent of women living in urban and suburban communities.

According to the Federal Bureau of Investigation (FBI) the number of forcible rapes reported to law enforcement in 2003 declined in every population group in the nation with the exception of communities of 25,000 to 49,999 where reports increased by 3.2 percent and communities of under 10,000 where reports increased by 3.7 percent.

Overall, forcible rapes reported to law enforcement in 2003 declined by 1.9 percent from 2002.

According to FBI statistics there were 95,136 forcible rapes of females in 2002, representing a 4.7 percent increase from the previous year.

Arrests for forcible rape in 2002 were estimated at 28,288.

An average of 140,990 completed rapes, 109,230 attempted rapes, and 152,680 completed and attempted sexual assaults were committed against persons age 12 or older in the United States between the years 1992 and 2000 [according to the U.S. Department of Justice].

The majority of adolescent sexual assaults (86 percent) went unreported.

Rape Reporting Rates

Only 36 percent of completed rapes were reported to the police during the years 1992 to 2000. Thirty-four percent of the attempted rapes, and 26 percent of the completed and attempted sexual assaults were reported.

A recently published eight-year study indicates that when perpetrators of completed rape are current or former husbands or boyfriends, the crimes go unreported to the police 77 percent of the time. When the perpetrators are friends or acquaintances, the rapes go unreported 61 percent of the time. When the perpetrators are strangers, the rapes go unreported 54 percent of the time.

A recent report based on the 1995 National Survey of Adolescents (NSA) found that 13 percent of girls and 3.4 percent of boys surveyed had been sexually assaulted.

Of the sexual assault victims in the NSA, 74 percent reported that the assault was committed by someone they knew well. Almost one-third (32.5 percent) of sexual assault cases involved perpetrators who were friends, 21.1 percent were committed by a family member, and 23.2 percent were committed by strangers.

Slightly more than one in four sexual assault victims (28.1 percent) said they feared death or serious injury during the sexual assault.

The majority of adolescent sexual assaults (86 percent) went unreported.

[According to a 2003 U.S. Department of Justice report,] offenders perceived to be using drugs and/or alcohol committed about two in five rapes/sexual assaults against college students.

Between 1995–2000, 86 percent of all rapes/sexual assaults committed against college students were not reported to police, compared to 12 percent that were reported.

Prison Violence Is a Serious Problem for Women

Amnesty International

Amnesty International is a worldwide organization that campaigns for internationally recognized human rights to be respected and protected.

"That was not part of my sentence, to . . . perform oral sex with the officers."

New York prisoner Tanya Ross, November 1998.

This report describes violations of the internationally guaranteed human rights of women incarcerated in *prisons* and *jails* in the United States of America. The violations include rape and other forms of sexual abuse; the cruel, inhuman and degrading use of restraints on incarcerated women who are pregnant or seriously ill; inadequate access to treatment for physical and mental health needs; and confinement in isolation for prolonged periods in conditions of reduced sensory stimulation.

Amnesty International calls on the federal and state and local governments and authorities at all levels to take urgent action to ensure that the laws, regulations, policies and practices for which they are responsible rigorously conform to international standards and respect the human rights of women deprived of their liberty.

US Resistance to International Human Rights Commitments

The USA has played a leading role in the development of the international system of human rights protection over the past

"'Not Part of My Sentence:' Violations of the Human Rights of Women in Custody," *United States of America: Rights for All*, 2007. Reproduced by permission.

37

50 years. However, it has been reluctant to submit itself to international human rights law and to accept the same minimum standards for its own conduct that it demands from other countries.

The USA has declined to ratify key human rights treaties, it has reserved the right not to implement important provisions of treaties that it has ratified and has refused to permit people within the USA to bring complaints about alleged violations of their human rights to international monitoring bodies. . . .

Many authorities have not adapted their facilities and services to meet the particular needs of female inmates and have often treated them more poorly than male inmates.

Recommendations on Acceptance of International Human Rights Standards

The USA's reluctance to fully accept international human rights treaties and standards denies women in the USA rights and protections which the great majority of governments have agreed to recognise. The USA should:

- Ratify without reservations the Convention on the Elimination of All Forms of Discrimination Against Women

- Withdraw its reservations to the International Covenant on Civil and Political Rights and the Convention against Torture

- Give people in the USA the right to request the international human rights protection mechanisms established under the ICCPR (the Human Rights Committee) and the Convention against Torture (the

Committee against Torture) to consider complaints brought by individuals that the government has violated its obligations under the treaties.

Profile of Women in Custody

There are around 138,000 women in jails and prisons in the USA, more than three times the number of women who were incarcerated in 1985. Much of the increase is due to the so-called "war on drugs" conducted by federal and state government criminal justice authorities since the 1980s. About 40 percent of women in prison have been imprisoned for violating drug laws; only about 25 percent are in prison because they have committed a violent crime.

One of the most striking characteristics of incarcerated women is that the proportion who are of racial and ethnic minority background greatly exceeds their representation in the general population. The rate of imprisonment of black women is more than eight times the rate of imprisonment of white women; the rate of imprisonment of Hispanic women is nearly four times the rate of imprisonment of white women. The "war on drugs" has had a disproportionate impact on racial and ethnic minority women. For example, in New York, 77 percent of Hispanic female prisoners and, 59 percent of black female prisoners are incarcerated for drug offences, compared with 34 percent of white female prisoners.

For more than a decade, the number of women in prison and jails has increased at a faster rate than the increase in the rate at which men are being incarcerated but women still form only a small proportion—about eight percent—of the incarcerated population in the USA. Because women are such a minority, many authorities have not adapted their facilities and services to meet the particular needs of female inmates and have often treated them more poorly than male inmates. . . .

Sexual Abuse

I'm tired of being gynaecologically examined every time I'm searched. *Inmate at Valley State Prison for Women, California, speaking with an Amnesty International delegate, November 1998, about how some male guards conduct searches*

Many women in prisons and jails in the USA are victims of rape and other forms of sexual abuse including, commonly, sexually offensive language; male staff touching female inmates' breasts and genitals while conducting searches and male staff watching women while they are naked.

These are some reports received by Amnesty International relating to the period 1997–99:

- Guards who were later dismissed or disciplined were found to have sexually abused female inmates in jails and prisons in Florida, Idaho, Illinois, Maryland, New Hampshire, Maryland, Michigan, Ohio, Texas, Virginia, West Virginia and Wyoming.

- The US Justice Department initiated legal action against the states of Arizona and Michigan following investigations into state prisons that found evidence of systematic sexual abuse including sexual assault and male guards who, "without good reason," watched female inmates dressing, showering and using the toilet.

- Prisoners and other sources reported that inmates were the victims of sexual abuse by staff at Valley State Prison for Women in California. Amnesty International delegates interviewed prisoners at the prison in November 1998 and were told that some male officers watched the women while they were dressing and undressing and, in breach of the approved procedure, touched prisoners' breasts and genitals when searching them.

- In March 1998, the Federal Bureau of Prisons agreed to pay three women a total of $500,000 to settle a lawsuit in which they claimed that correctional staff in federal institutions in California had committed and facilitated rape and other forms of sexual abuse against them between August and November 1995. The complaint included allegations that staff allowed male inmates to enter the women's cells in exchange for money and/or other favours and intimidated the women after they complained about their treatment.

Under international law, rape of an inmate by staff is considered to be torture. Other forms of sexual abuse violate the internationally recognized prohibition on cruel, inhuman or degrading treatment or punishment. Rape and sexual assault violate US federal and state criminal laws. In addition, 36 states, the District of Columbia and the federal government have laws specifically prohibiting sexual relations between staff and inmates. A number of the laws prohibit staff-inmate sexual contact regardless of inmate consent, recognizing that such sexual relations cannot be truly consensual because of the power that staff have over inmates. Fourteen states do not have laws criminalizing sexual relations between staff and inmates. . . .

Restraints

The doctor came and said that yes, this baby is coming right now, and started to prepare the bed for delivery. Because I was shackled to the bed, they couldn't remove the lower part of the bed for the delivery, and they couldn't put my feet in the stirrups. My feet were still shackled together, and I couldn't get my legs apart. The doctor called for the officer, but the officer had gone down the hall. No one else could unlock the shackles, and my baby was coming but I couldn't open my legs . . . Finally the officer came and unlocked the shackles from my ankles. My baby was born then. I stayed in the delivery room with my baby for a little while, but then the officer put the leg shackles and handcuffs back on me and I was taken out of the delivery room.

"Maria Jones" describing how she gave birth
while an inmate of Cook County Jail, Chicago, 1998.

Around the USA, it is common for restraints to be used on sick and pregnant incarcerated women when they are transported to and kept in hospital, regardless of whether they have a history of violence (which only a minority have) and regardless of whether they have ever absconded or attempted to escape (which few women have).

One women reported that she gave birth alone in the labour room as she screamed and lay handcuffed to the bed.

On 18 November, 1998, Amnesty International delegates visited Madera County Hospital in California, where female prisoners are taken when they are seriously ill or in labour and for a short period after giving birth. The ward is locked. Inside the ward are four armed guards. Yet every inmate is chained by a leg to her bed. An inmate showed the Amnesty International delegates her shackle. She could lie on her side but she could not roll over.

The New York City Department of Corrections' policy prohibits the use of restraints on pregnant inmates admitted to hospital for delivery "unless the inmate attempts to escape at the hospital or the inmate engages in violent behaviour at the hospital which presents a danger of injury." However, Amnesty International has received reports that six New York City prisoners, none of whom had attempted to escape or had a history of violence, were restrained while in hospital for delivery in 1998. One woman reported that she gave birth alone in the labour room as she screamed and lay handcuffed to the bed. Another woman reported that she was shackled to the bed after the birth of her baby by caesarian section even though a doctor had requested that, because of her surgery, she be allowed to walk around. This is the report provided of how another of the women was treated:

> While inducing her labor she was put into handcuffs. They took the handcuffs off when the baby was about to be born. After the baby was born she was shackled in the recovery room. She was shackled while she held the baby. Had to walk with shackles when she went to the baby. She asked the officer to hold the baby while she went to pick something up. The officer said it was against the rules. She had to manoeuvre with the shackles and the baby to pick up the item. In the room she had a civilian roommate and the roommate had visitors and she had to cover the shackles, she said she felt so ashamed. . . . She said she was traumatized and humiliated by the shackles. She was shackled when she saw her baby in the hospital nursery (a long distance from the room). Passing visitors were staring and making remarks. She was shackled when she took a shower; only one time when she was not.

Inmates have died because essential medical services were restricted in order to save money.

Amnesty International considers that there is no sound reason for authorities to routinely shackle and handcuff pregnant women or women who have just given birth and who are under armed guard. The use of restraints in these circumstances is cruel and degrading. It also endangers the woman and her child, as described by physician Dr Patricia Garcia

> Women in labor need to be mobile so that they can assume various positions as needed and so they can quickly be moved to an operating room. Having the woman in shackles compromises the ability to manipulate her legs into the

proper position for necessary treatment. The mother and baby's health could be compromised if there were complications during delivery, such as haemorrhage or decrease in fetal heart tones. . . .

Health

On the night of April 20th, 1997, Arizona jail inmate Annette Romo, who was pregnant, began bleeding. "I told the guard and she said medical was not in at that time of night and there was nothing she could do. As the night went on the bleeding got worse and so did my stomach ache. I didn't sleep at all that night and when the guard passed by me I was crying and I told her the bleeding was getting worse and that I couldn't stand the stomach cramps I was having. She again told me there was nothing she could do." Annette Romo's bleeding continued through the night and the next day, when she collapsed and was rushed to hospital and underwent surgery. "I still to this day have dreams about what happened . . . It was the worst thing I have ever experienced. If they would have only helped me when I first asked all this would not have happened nor would I have had to lose my baby."

Letter to Amnesty International, 22 February, 1998.

International standards specify that medical care must be provided to people who are detained or imprisoned whenever necessary, free of charge. The US Supreme Court has also ruled that inmates have a right to adequate medical care for serious medical needs. Despite these international and national legal standards, many prisons and jails have failed to provide adequate health care. . . .

Perhaps the most commonly cited barrier to effective access to health services by incarcerated women is that prisons and jails employ too few medical staff. As a consequence, inmates have to wait lengthy periods to be seen initially and to receive follow-up care. Some may not be seen at all. In a recent national jail survey, fewer than half the women received a medical examination to determine their health status after they were taken into custody.

Women who receive treatment also experience significant and serious delays in ongoing medical supervision and follow-up care. In a 1996 study of women in prison in California, Florida and Connecticut, 42 percent of women receiving medication for physical disorders, and 31 percent of those receiving treatment for mental health disorders reported that they were not receiving medical supervision. The effects of the lack of medical supervision, the study noted, included "physical deterioration of prisoners with chronic and degenerative diseases, such as kidney disease and cancer, and over medication of prisoners with psychotropic drugs, resulting in lethargy and/or problems with speech and gait (shuffling)."

Another common barrier to medical attention is that inmates in many prisons and jails must obtain the permission of non-medical staff in order to be attended by a doctor. Prisoners and lawyers have told Amnesty International of cases where non-medical staff refused permission because they thought a prisoner was lying about her condition, or delayed calling for medical assistance because they did not think immediate attention was warranted.

In violation of international standards, many prisons and jails charge inmates for medical attention. Although inmates who have no money are exempt, charges may deter poor prisoners from seeking help for what might be serious matters. Prisoners interviewed by Amnesty International in California said that the payment requirement is a significant deterrent for women who have a small amount of money, even those who have prison jobs for which the maximum rate of pay is 33 cents per hour.

In some states, private companies have taken over prison health services. There have been a number of reports that inmates have died because essential medical services were restricted in order to save money. For example, in 1996 Melody

Bird, an inmate in Pinellas County Jail, Florida, complained of serious chest pains and difficulty breathing. Nurses at the jail believed she was having a heart attack but were not permitted to call for an ambulance to take an inmate to hospital without prior approval from the medical director of the company contracted to provide health care services at the jail. They contacted the medical director but did not receive permission to call an ambulance for 13 hours. Melody Bird died before reaching the emergency room. After her death, it is reported, "company nurses came forward to say that they had been pressured to avoid sending inmates to the emergency room because of the expense." As well, it was discovered that the company sometimes paid the medical director bonuses to keep inmates out of the emergency room. Several authorities are reported to have ended contracts with private companies because of concerns that their services were of poor quality.

Violence Against Immigrant Women Is a Serious Problem

Jan Schakowsky

Jan Schakowsky has served as U.S. Representative for Illinois since 1998 and is a leading advocate for women's issues in Congress. She delivered the following speech on July 7, 2005, to promote her bill, the Immigrant Victims of Violence Protection Act.

I'm proud to be here today [July 7, 2005] with so many advocates who are fighting every day on behalf of immigrants and domestic violence victims. I want to first thank Heartland Alliance's Midwest Immigrant & Human Rights Center for your work on behalf of low-income and impoverished immigrants, refugees, and asylum seekers and for the generous use of your space. And I want to especially recognize the two women who have courageously joined us here to tell their stories about being trapped in abusive relationships and being victims of our flawed legal system. They know from personal experience that there is an urgent need to change the law to save the lives of immigrant women across America.

The Special Situation of Immigrant Women

Domestic violence affects families and communities throughout our country, but its impact upon immigrant communities is especially devastating. Many women who have immigrated to America do not have control over their own immigration status—their spouse does. And when their spouse turns violent, immigrant women face a decision they should never have to make: They can leave their spouse and face deportation and separation from their children, or they can stay in an abusive

Jan Schakowsky, "Schakowsky Joins Advocates, Victims for Press Conference in Support of Her New Bill to Protect Immigrant Women from Domestic Violence," http://www.house.gov, July 7, 2005.

relationship in order to protect their immigration status and risk losing their lives in the process.

It's critical that Congress provide new protections for immigrants as it considers reauthorizing the Violence Against Women Act.

These women need help. We must remove the perverse incentive in our laws for women to stay in abusive relationships. And we must erase the double standard that allows women who are American citizens to escape their abusive spouse but uproots immigrant women in America from their families and their communities when they flee an abusive spouse.

Last Thursday [June 30, 2005] I was joined by 77 original co-sponsors . . . to introduce a bill called the Immigrant Victims of Violence Protection Act, which would offer new protections to immigrant women trapped in abusive relationships. This bill offers immigrant women who leave their abusive spouses the same legal protections they would have had in a healthy relationship.

Helping Vulnerable Victims

Today we will hear from two victims who were helped by organizations in Chicago to escape their abusers with their lives intact. While they were fortunate to have found advocates to guide them through the immigration process, there are others whose spouses still threaten deportation as a punishment. Under current law the Department of Homeland Security [DHS] could still act on these abusers' threats, and deport these victims of domestic violence. My bill would create a sanctuary for these victims and prevent DHS from seizing them in domestic violence shelters, rape crisis centers, and protection order courts. Any victim who can prove they've been subjected to domestic violence would be protected from deportation under this legislation. The bill would also provide a safety net for battered legal immigrants and their children by allowing them access to health insurance, food, work permits, and other social services essential to their economic well-being. With these increased protections, immigrant women will be empowered to live on their own as legal residents, free from abuse.

Over the next few months Congress will consider reauthorizing the Violence Against Women Act [VAWA]. Originally passed in 1994, this landmark legislation made significant progress in reducing violence against immigrant women. But there are still many women and children whose lives are in danger today. Many victims of domestic violence, sexual assault, child abuse or trafficking are leaving abusive relationships only to be deported and separated from their families. Others remain economically trapped by abusers or traffickers in life-threatening environments.

It's critical that Congress provide new protections for immigrants as it considers reauthorizing the Violence Against Women Act. Inclusion of my bill, or any that advances this cause, in the broader VAWA legislation would go a long way toward improving our policy. Women across this country, regardless of their immigration status, should never have to choose to remain in an abusive relationship in order to avoid deportation or separation from their children. In the land of the free, too many immigrant women are being trapped in their own homes, their lives and possibly their children's lives endangered by an abusive spouse. The time to lift the legal barriers keeping immigrant women in abusive relationships is long overdue.

Violence Against Women Has Been Exaggerated by Feminists

Neil Boyd

Neil Boyd is a professor at Simon Fraser University where he teaches courses related to law, crime, and criminal justice policy.

Since 1949 and the publication of George Orwell's [famous book] *1984*, there has been a concern within our culture about the metaphorical ruler that Orwell termed Big Brother, the supreme leader of the "Party" that effectively created conformity and stifled freedom of speech, thought, and action. Orwell's Big Brother has become a part of our language, a shorthand for government tyranny. In the last twenty-five years we have seen the gradual emergence of a different kind of tyranny—the rule of Big Sister.

The Rise of Big Sister

Big Sister is far afield from the vitally important feminism of my youth. During the 1960s and 1970s, we rightly argued for a woman's right to choose, for equality in the workplace, and for the equal rights of gays and lesbians; these remain as important accomplishments and continuing struggles. Big Sister does not represent equality. She is, rather, a powerful voice at the margins of feminism, promoting division, deception, and bad science. Like Big Brother, she has stifled freedom of thought, speech, and action, but she has done it in ways that we have been slow to recognize. We have been told by her that male sexuality is inevitably predatory—that pornography is the theory and rape is the practice. Big Sister suggests that male-female differences in sexual response and expression are wholly the product of our culture and that women should be offended by these differences.

Discussions about sexuality are limited in subtle and not so subtle ways. Males' interest in the physical appearance of females is characterized by Big Sister as "objectification"—a focus on the body that encourages men to see women as sexual objects. Objectification then leads men to behave inappropriately toward women—to subject them to unwanted sexual advances.

The mantra of many extreme feminists that women never lie about their victimization is simply absurd.

Women are urged to fight the "patriarchal domination" inherent in objectification as it is the first step on the road to sexual harassment, and worse. It is heresay to suggest that objectification—finding pleasure in the body and its most typically sexual parts—isn't harmful to women. Although researchers have repeatedly demonstrated that women are more likely to be sexually aroused by written materials and men by visual depictions of sexuality, Big Sister isn't listening. She views these long-established differences as proof of a culturally imposed male sexual aggression, despite the consistent finding that different routes and inclinations for male and female sexual arousal appear to have their origins in biology, not culture. To invoke biology as a possible explanation for differences in sexual expression is to invite characterization by Big Sister as an apologist for the continuance of patriarchy.

Radical Feminism

Such politically and ideologically driven conceptions of our sexuality were conceived during the past few decades, primarily by self-described radical feminists in departments of women's studies, law, and sociology. These feminists and their heirs can be found in virtually every university in North America. The reason for the existence of their way of thinking has little to do with research and scholarship, and everything to do with political power and the politics of guilt. Although it does make sense to study gender relations, sexuality, and law, or changing social constructions of what we might call family life, the agenda, especially in women's studies, is avowedly political.

Departments of women's studies arose in response to the historic exclusion of women from social, political, and academic life; they were designed to acknowledge women as a crucial part of the academy. Although many who inhabit these structures today produce excellent scholarship, the existence of their departments is no longer justifiable. Not only is there no clear theory of the building of knowledge that can legitimate the creation of this new field (unless it were situated under a wider umbrella of gender studies or the study of sexuality), there is no longer any relevant political justification. Women have taken their rightful place in academia. There is no systematic exclusion of women from the halls of higher learning or from any other important avenue of social or intellectual life in North America.

Radical Laws

The greatest damage inflicted by radical feminism has occurred in the rewriting of law regarding sexual and gender relations. . . . Pro-censorship feminists have argued successfully for the criminal prohibition of obscenity, a prohibition that has been used against the consensual sex of minorities—specifically, against consensual sex among gays and lesbians. The law of sexual harassment, unknown a generation ago, is now well established, but with a frighteningly inadequate burden of proof and a dangerously vague test of liability.

The mantra of many extreme feminists that women never lie about their victimization is simply absurd when considered logically, and it has led to significant injustices across North America. An unhappy or even unfulfilling sexual experience can now be reinterpreted as sexual harassment or sexual assault.... And the law now allows the subjective perception of a "hostile working environment" to be the basis for a finding of sexual harassment, even if sexual harassment is not the focus of the so-called hostile environment.

Big Sister has mischaracterized the nature and exaggerated the extent of domestic violence in our culture. You have likely heard the claim that one in every three women in domestic relationships will at some point in her lifetime be the victim of a male batterer. What you probably didn't know is that the Big Sister definition of battering includes even such minor physical encounters as pushing, restraining, or pinching. These constitute aggression, certainly, but battering?

Big Sister also urges mandatory arrest in all cases of domestic violence, even though the best evidence reveals that failing to give both abused women and police any discretion can, in some circumstances, lead to greater risks of future violence by the male perpetrator. But taking a "zero tolerance" approach to domestic violence has a political cachet: "Domestic violence is a crime like all others and should be prosecuted as such." But domestic violence is not a crime like all others, and depriving a woman of the right to determine whether charges are laid against an intimate partner can be an act of condescension and a usurping of her power rather than an act of support for the rights of battered women....

The public perspective on ... free expression, sexual harassment, sexual assault, and domestic conflict has been transformed, primarily by an ideologically intolerant network of women (and some men) who call themselves feminists. Those who critique their work are denounced as sexist, antifeminist, homophobic, and masculinist. When Big Sister is at her least tolerant she labels her opponents in the most egregious terms: obstructers of justice, harassers of women and children, perpetrators of sex crimes, and shielders of such perpetrators. The sexual landscape of our daily lives is now dotted with potentially explosive mines.

U.S. Policy to Reduce Violence Against Women Creates Injustice Instead

Respecting Accuracy in Domestic Abuse Reporting (RADAR)

Respecting Accuracy in Domestic Abuse Reporting is a nonprofit, nonpartisan organization of men and women working to improve the effectiveness of the U.S.'s approach to solving domestic violence. Excerpted from Respecting Accuracy in Domestic Abuse Reporting, "A Culture of False Accusations: How VAWA Harms Families and Children," RADAR Web site at www.mediaradar.org, 2007. For the complete and unabridged version of this report, including extensive supporting footnotes, see http://www.mediaradar.org/docs/VAWA-A-Culture-of-False-Allegations.pdf.

Families are the cornerstone of a free society and provide the environment in which children are nurtured and protected. While domestic violence occurs in some dysfunctional families, governmental efforts to stem domestic violence have created a whole raft of new problems. Although driven by good intentions, the Violence Against Women Act has established a legal framework which creates perverse incentives, thus encouraging the making of false claims of abuse, escalating partner conflict, and discouraging partner reconciliation. The result is that, in the name of stopping domestic violence, government policies break up non-violent families and separate children from innocent, loving, non-violent parents.

There are many factors that create an environment that encourages the making of false allegations of domestic violence:

Respecting Accuracy in Domestic Abuse Reporting, "A Culture of False Accusations: How VAWA Harms Families and Children," RADAR Web site at *Mediaradar.org* Web site, 2007. http://www.mediaradar.org/docs/VAWA-A-Culture-of-False-Allegations.pdf.

1. Current laws define domestic violence in such broad and ambiguous terms that almost any action, violent or not, is counted as "violence". Thus, David Letterman was subjected to a temporary restraining order because a viewer claimed he'd been harassing her telepathically for a decade.

2. In most states, laws provide "remedies" to persons who claim to be abuse victims without requiring any proof that abuse occurred, and with no penalties for perjury. This creates powerful incentives for people to make false claims in order to reap the benefits of those remedies. In various states, those benefits can include sole control of the family residence, reimbursement for attorney's fees, sole custody of the children, etc.

3. Left to their own devices, most couples are able to resolve disagreements on their own without anything that the average person would call "violence". But the overbroad redefinition of "violence" mentioned above, when combined with the mandatory-arrest and no-drop prosecution policies now in effect in most states, make it nearly impossible for couples to resolve their differences once the authorities have gotten involved.

4. Many states have enacted laws that have the effect of denying any form of child custody to anyone accused of domestic violence. In many states, simply claiming to be fearful can be sufficient to remove the other parent's child visitation rights.

5. The Violence Against Women Act funds judicial education programs that are ideological and one-sided. In one such program, N.J. Judge Richard Russell was caught on tape telling incoming family court judges, "Your job is not to become concerned about all the constitutional rights of the man that you're violating as you grant a restraining order. Throw him out on the street, give him the clothes on his back, and tell him, 'See ya' around.'"

The above factors create a nexus that gives rise to all-too-common allegations of domestic "violence" in which no violence actually occurred.

Criminal Law

Each year about one million persons are arrested under criminal law for intimate partner violence, of whom 77% are male. A disproportionate number of arrestees are Black. One report by the Ms. Foundation for Women expressed the concern that overly aggressive law enforcement has led to "mass incarceration of men, especially young men of color, decimating marginalized communities."

In the past the officers would intervene or separate the parties to let them cool off. Now these cases end up in criminal courts.

Many persons assume a criminal charge of domestic violence [DV] involves an actual assault. But about one-third of domestic violence criminal prosecutions do not arise from a physical attack. One analysis in New York City found that 15% of the cases that went to criminal court involved criminal contempt (typically arising from restraining order violations) and 20% included crimes such as harassment, criminal mischief, and larceny.

It is not known how many domestic violence arrests involve allegations that are frivolous or false, but one former DV prosecutor in Georgia wrote, "As politically incorrect as it is to say, many women file charges against boyfriends/spouses on a routine basis, and then recant the charges when the cases come to trial. Some of the alleged perpetrators are really guilty, and [a] *very large percentage (though not majority) are not guilty of anything except making the woman in their life angry.*" [italics added].

Or a person can be arrested for simply acting in self-defense:

> Lisa Ortiz attacked her boyfriend, Baltimore Orioles pitcher Scott Erickson, by throwing objects at him. To protect himself, Erickson carried Ortiz out of his apartment. Even though Ortiz suffered no injuries, the police arrested Erickson. Ortiz later admitted that Erickson "has never been physically abusive toward me, and in no way do I feel threatened or have I felt fear from Scott."

A significant number of criminal prosecutions for domestic violence do not include any allegation of physical "violence," and some claims are actually frivolous and false.

A vindictive motive can be discerned in some cases:

> "Sally" of Vallejo, California, had been ordered by the court to vacate the family home. But the day she was supposed to move out, she accused her husband "Joe" of pushing her. Joe spent the night in jail. The judge later dismissed the charges. "Even the cop was apologetic," said Joe. "She told me she didn't believe (my wife), but that she had to arrest me because the accusation had been made."

Two New York City attorneys have claimed the local police policy is to "arrest everyone and let the prosecutor sort 'em out." Whatever happened to the legal requirement for "probable cause"?

Thus, a significant number of criminal prosecutions for domestic violence do not include any allegation of physical "violence," and some claims are actually frivolous and false.

Civil Law

It has been noted that allegations of domestic violence tend to cluster around partners with children and no prior history of violence. Such domestic violence allegations are made to gain a legal advantage during a divorce proceeding, many believe. With remarkable candor, one legal expert advised, "With child abuse and spouse abuse you don't have to prove anything. You just have to accuse."

These tactics have become so widespread that divorce lawyers euphemistically refer to them as "silver bullets," "slam-dunks," or "divorce planning." Legal commentators have expressed alarm over the perversion of justice:

- Elaine Epstein, former president of the Massachusetts Bar Association, once revealed, "Everyone knows that restraining orders and orders to vacate are granted to virtually all who apply . . . In many cases, allegations of abuse are now used for tactical advantage."

- In California, the State Bar admits that protective orders are "almost routinely issued by the court in family law proceedings, even when there is relatively meager evidence and usually without notice to the restrained person . . . it is troubling that they appear to be sought more and more frequently for retaliation and litigation purposes."

- New Jersey attorney David Heleniak sums up the process this way: "In ten days, the hypothetical husband has gone from having a normal life with a wife, children and home to being a social pariah, homeless, poor, and alone trapped in a Kafkaesque nightmare."

By any common-sense definition, "violence" involves the perpetration of a physical assault that may result in injury. Each year 2–3 million civil restraining orders are issued in the United States. But analyses by the Massachusetts Trial Court and others reveal that half of those orders are not based on even an *allegation* of physical violence.

Thus each year, at least one million false allegations of domestic violence are filed under civil law—often with serious consequences for families and children.

Impact on Families

The current epidemic of domestic violence claims weakens the American family by promoting family dissolution and discouraging men from marriage.

Family Dissolution Our nation's domestic violence system often portrays intact families as violent, escalates partner conflict, imposes separation, thwarts reconciliation, leads to divorce, and blocks pro-family reform.

1. Portrays Intact Families as Violent: According to the Department of Justice, only 2% of DV incidents involve currently married couples who live together. But the domestic violence industry often makes dishonest claims such as, "women are safer in the streets than they are in their own homes." Likewise, training videos and TV documentaries (such as Lifetime's *Terror at Home*) often depict domestic violence as a problem mostly of married couples.

As a result of aggressive law-enforcement and prosecution efforts, our nation's domestic violence system amounts to 'state-imposed de facto *divorce . . ."*

---

2. Escalates Partner Conflict: In the past, police intervention encouraged the parties to calm down and made amends. But now, a call to the police has the opposite effect. One former prosecutor in Ohio notes, "In the past the officers would intervene or separate the parties to let them cool off. Now these cases end up in criminal courts. It's exacerbating tensions between the parties, and it's turning law-abiding citizens into criminals."

Indeed under the laws of most states, any marital tiff can be considered domestic "abuse" and a single incident of physical aggression can be deemed to be full-scale battering. "There are cases of pushing and shoving that are treated like crimes of the century," relates California attorney John Digicianto. Thus, state intrusion into the matter only serves to heighten the dispute.

3. *Imposes Separation*: One California assistant public defender complains that "the district attorney pushes a particular point of view: separation." Likewise, women's shelters, sometimes criticized as "one-stop divorce shops," discourage clients from reuniting with their partners, even when the abuse is minor.

One woman's account illustrates how a shelter's false police report impacted the family:

> Following several heated arguments with her husband, Susan went to her local shelter to get counseling for herself. She emphasized to the shelter worker there had been no physical violence.
>
> Nonetheless, the shelter called the police. The police report stated—falsely—that Susan's husband had threatened to rape her and to kill the children. As a result, the husband was ordered out of his house.
>
> Two days later, the Child and Protective Services worker came to the house and detained the children, claiming the mother had not adequately protected her children. The children were placed in foster care for 38 days.
>
> Then Susan's husband was arrested and bail was set at $350,000. Because he worked as a truck driver, he couldn't afford an attorney. So he agreed to a plea bargain with 3 years probation—even though no physical violence had ever occurred.

4. *Thwarts Reconciliation*: VAWA [Violence Against Women Act]-endorsed treatment programs likewise stymie reconciliation. One analysis of 30 states that have implemented standards for offender treatment programs found that 42% of states actually prohibit couple's counseling.

A study by the National Institute for Justice observed, "Restrictions on couples therapy and individual psychotherapy for battering are a point of contention between feminist-oriented batterer intervention providers and mental health providers in many communities."

5. *Leads to Divorce*: As a result of aggressive law-enforcement and prosecution efforts, our nation's domestic violence system amounts to "state-imposed *de facto* divorce," explains Harvard Law School professor Jeannie Suk. The government "initiates and dictates the end of the intimate relationship as a solution to DV."

6. *Blocks Pro-Family Reform*: Efforts to reform divorce laws or promote marriage are often opposed by domestic violence industry advocates at both the state and national levels.

Men Reluctant to Commit

Most young women hope to eventually settle down and get married. But given the number of fathers who have lost their homes and children to false allegations of domestic violence, it is not surprising that many single men are now opting to forego family life altogether.

According to a national Rutgers University survey, 22% of single heterosexual American men 25–34 years old indicate that they do not plan to ever marry. And 53% of these men say that they are "not interested in getting married anytime soon."

These figures translate into many millions of families that will never come into existence. In sum, there is very little that is family-friendly in our nation's domestic violence system.

Effects on Children

More than one million American children experience divorce each year. How often is a false allegation of DV made during the course of the divorce proceeding?

One study of divorcing couples with custody disputes found that DV allegations were made in 55% of the cases, 59% of which could not be substantiated as true. Thus, each year, many thousands of children experience divorces in which false allegations of partner violence are made, allegations that often serve as the basis to deprive children of contact from one of their parents.

The chances that a young male will engage in criminal activity doubles if he is raised without a father.

Even after the divorce, allegations of domestic abuse may be used to separate children from a parent:

My ex-wife used a domestic violence charge against me so that she could take the children out of state. It worked great for her. The judge automatically granted a restraining order so that I had to stay away from her and my children (no more visits with my children). My ex-wife had no proof and actually told the judge that I was OK but she didn't like my [new] wife.

After a year and 25K [twenty-five thousand dollars] in expenses, and almost losing my job and my license for being an accused domestic violence offender, I gave in and let her take my children out of state. And she agreed to drop the charges.

The all-too-common result of these laws is a weakening or severing of the child-parent bond. "I've run into hundreds of fathers who've been falsely accused of domestic violence and can't see their children because of it," notes shared-parenting proponent Teri Stoddard. These non-custodial fathers experience a range of emotional and psychological problems, ranging from a sense of displacement and loss, depression, and even suicide.

Four decades ago, Daniel Patrick Moynihan foresaw the impact of fatherless families:

From the wild Irish slums of the 19th century eastern seaboard to the riot-torn suburbs of Los Angeles, there is one unmistakable lesson in American history: A community that allows a large number of young men to grow up in broken families, dominated by women, never acquiring any stable relationship to male authority, never acquiring any rational expectations about the future—that community asks for and gets chaos.

Moynihan's prediction is now confirmed by dozens of studies that gauge the effects of separating children from their fathers. These are some highlights:

Child Abuse

As discussed above, most states have enacted laws that restrict shared parenting, based on the belief that abusive husbands are also likely to be abusive fathers. However, the advocates of such laws rarely mention that the perpetrators of child mistreatment and homicide are more likely to be mothers than fathers—not because women are more abusive, but because single parents, who are usually mothers, lack the social supports that intact families have.

Extensive research shows that when a couple separates, the risk of physical and sexual child abuse increases dramatically. For example, one national survey found that 7.4% of children who lived with one parent had ever been sexually abused, compared to only 4.2% of children living with both parents.

The most recent National Incidence Study (NIS) of Child Abuse and Neglect found that, compared to children living with both parents, children living with a single parent were placed at substantially higher risk of abuse. These children have a:

- 64% greater risk of experiencing emotional neglect

- 165% greater risk of experiencing physical neglect

- 77% greater risk of being harmed by physical abuse

- Approximately 80% greater risk of suffering *serious* injury or harm from abuse or neglect

But these statistics actually *understate* the risk, because the NIS combines co-habiting and married parents into one group—and child abuse is substantially higher among co-habiting parents.

A better gauge of the risk that single parenthood places on children comes from a large British study. The research found that, compared to married biological parents, children with single mothers have a 14-fold higher risk of experiencing *serious* child abuse, and a 7-fold higher risk of suffering *fatal* child abuse.

Other Indicators of Child Welfare

Children who live apart from their fathers are at risk for a broad range of social pathologies, including educational, behavioral, and health problems:

School performance:

- Academic performance: A study of Black children ages 6–9 showed that children living with both parents scored significantly higher on tests of intellectual ability than children in mother-only households.

- School drop-out rates: Fatherless children are twice as likely to drop out of school.

- School disciplinary problems: Only 13% of 6th to 12th graders living with both parents have had behavior problems that resulted in suspension or expulsion, compared to 27% who lived in mother-only families.

Behavioral issues:

- Among young adolescents, only 10% living with both parents had had sexual relations, compared to 23% who lived with a single mother.

- Suicide: Only 9% of high school students from intact families reported suicidal behavior, compared to 20% of teens from single-parent homes.

Health:

- Injuries: A study of 17,110 children showed that children who lived with their divorced mothers had risks of injury that were 20–30% higher than children who lived with both biological parents.

- Longevity: Children who experienced parental divorce had a lifespan 4 years shorter than children who did not experience divorce.

Poverty:

- In 1999, the poverty rate for children living in single-mother families was 50%, compared to only 9% of children in married-couple families.

- During the first 4 months of a father's absence, the chances that the child's family would fall below the poverty line increased from 18.5% to 37.6%.

- Of all children in TANF (Temporary Assistance to Needy Families) families, 71.8% lived with a single parent in 1998.

Crime:

- Juvenile delinquency: The chances that a young male will engage in criminal activity doubles if he is raised without a father.

- Violent crime: Low percentages of father-absent households were associated with lower rates of homicide among black and white men.

Children Are Our Future

Some may dispute the value of aggressive law enforcement measures. Many believe that restraining orders are ineffective and even counter-productive. And there may be controversy as to whether the Violence Against Women Act can be credited for reducing overall levels of partner abuse.

But there can be little doubt that VAWA has contributed to our culture of false allegations. Each year, at least one million false allegations of domestic violence are made, often in the context of a divorce.

The resulting separation of children from one of their parents is linked to higher child abuse rates and the worsening of a broad range of indicators of child well-being. Any society that aspires to survive and prosper must be careful to place our children first.

False Rape Accusations by Women Are Common

Marc Angelucci and Glenn Sacks

Marc Angelucci is an attorney and the president of the Los Angeles chapter of the National Coalition of Free Men. Glenn Sacks is a men's and fathers' issues columnist, commentator, radio talk show host, and blogger.

Despite its many painful and unseemly aspects, the Kobe Bryant [a professional basketball player] rape case and the media storm surrounding it have drawn attention to a severely neglected problem: false rape accusations.

In her recent [September 2004 *San Francisco*] *Daily Journal* column, high profile feminist professor Wendy Murphy dismisses the problem of false accusations as an "ugly myth," and calls for "boiling rage" activism to address what she perceives as the anti-woman bias of the criminal justice system. Like many victims' advocates, Murphy cannot seem to fathom the possibility that Bryant could be innocent. However, research shows that false allegations of rape are frighteningly common.

According to a nine-year study conducted by former Purdue sociologist Eugene J. Kanin, in over 40 percent of the cases reviewed, the complainants eventually admitted that no rape had occurred. Kanin also studied rape allegations in two large Midwestern universities and found that 50 percent of the allegations were recanted by the accuser.

Accusers Admit to Lying

Kanin found that most of the false accusers were motivated by a need for an alibi or a desire for revenge. Kanin was once well known and lauded by the feminist movement for his groundbreaking research on male sexual aggression. His studies on false rape accusations, however, received very little attention.

Any honest veteran sex assault investigator will tell you that rape is one of the most falsely reported crimes.

Kanin's findings are hardly unique. In 1985 the Air Force conducted a study of 556 rape accusations. Over one quarter of the accusers admitted, either just before they took a lie detector test or after they had failed it, that no rape occurred. A further investigation by independent reviewers found that 60 percent of the original rape allegations were false.

The most common reasons the women gave for falsely accusing rape were "spite or revenge," and to compensate for feelings of guilt or shame.

A *Washington Post* investigation of rape reports in seven Virginia and Maryland counties in 1990 and 1991 found that nearly one in four were unfounded. When contacted by the *Post*, many of the alleged victims admitted that they had lied.

Other Evidence of False Allegations

It is true, of course, that not every accuser who recants had accused falsely. But it is also true that some who do not recant were not telling the truth.

According to a 1996 Department of Justice Report, of the roughly 10,000 sexual assault cases analyzed with DNA evidence over the previous seven years, 2,000 excluded the primary suspect, and another 2,000 were inconclusive. The report notes that these figures mirror an informal National Institute of Justice survey of private laboratories, and suggests that there exists "some strong, underlying systemic problems that generate erroneous accusations and convictions."

That false allegations are a major problem has been confirmed by several prominent prosecutors, including Linda

Fairstein, former head of the New York County District Attorney's Sex Crimes Unit. Fairstein, the author of *Sexual Violence: Our War Against Rape*, says, "there are about 4,000 reports of rape each year in Manhattan. Of these, about half simply did not happen."

Craig Silverman, a former Colorado prosecutor known for his zealous prosecution of rapists during his 16-year career, says that false rape accusations occur with "scary frequency." As a regular commentator on the Bryant trial for Denver's ABC affiliate, Silverman noted that "any honest veteran sex assault investigator will tell you that rape is one of the most falsely reported crimes." According to Silverman, a Denver sex-assault unit commander estimates that nearly half of all reported rape claims are false.

The Myth of Rare False Allegations

The media has largely ignored these studies and experts and has instead promoted the notion that only 2% of rape allegations are false. This figure was made famous by feminist Susan Brownmiller in her 1975 book *Against Our Will: Men, Women and Rape*. Brownmiller was relaying the alleged comments of a New York judge concerning the rate of false rape accusations in a New York City police precinct in 1974.

Potentially innocent men were prevented from properly defending themselves by the rape shield laws.

A 1997 *Columbia Journalism Review* analysis of rape statistics noted that the 2% statistic is often falsely attributed to the Federal Bureau of Investigation [FBI], and has no clear and credible study to support it. The FBI's statistic for "unfounded" rape accusations is 9%, but this definition only includes cases where the accuser recants or the evidence contradicts her story. Instances where the case is dismissed for lack of evidence are not included in the "unfounded" category.

Brownmiller's credibility can be assessed by her assertion in *Against Our Will* that rape is "nothing more or less than a conscious process of intimidation by which all men keep all women in a state of fear."

The Harm of Rape Shield Laws

Murphy also contends that the criminal justice system is stacked against women, and that the law reform initiatives promoted during the past three decades have "failed to make a bit of difference in the justice system's handling of rape cases." In reality, feminist advocacy and the now ubiquitous rape shield laws have made an enormous difference in the way the system treats rape cases

Some of these changes have been fair, and have led to greater protections for rape victims. However, others have made it more difficult for men to defend themselves, with at times horrifying consequences for the accused.

False accusations. . . are a form of psychological rape that can emotionally, socially, and economically destroy a person even if there is no conviction.

For example, in December [2003], the Arkansas Supreme Court denied an appeal by Ralph Taylor, who is serving a 13-year sentence for rape. The court held that evidence of the victim's alleged prior false allegations of rape was inadmissible because it was considered sexual conduct within the meaning of the state's rape shield statute. In that case, the defense proffered the testimony of two friends of the alleged victim, both of whom claimed that she had previously falsely accused another man of raping her. The court added that admitting such evidence could "inflame the jury."

In her book *Ceasefire: Why Women and Men Must Join Forces to Achieve True Equality, Boston Globe* columnist Cathy Young details numerous questionable rulings in which potentially innocent men were prevented from properly defending themselves by the rape shield laws which Murphy endorses.

One of these cases concerns an 18 year-old Wisconsin boy named Charles Steadman, who in 1993 was sentenced to eight years in prison for allegedly raping an older woman. Steadman was underage when the crime allegedly occurred, but was prohibited from revealing that his accuser was currently facing criminal charges of having sex with minors, and thus had an excellent reason to claim that the sex with Steadman was not consensual. Such evidence was deemed related to his accuser's sexual history and thus inadmissible.

In 1997, sportscaster Marv Albert was accused of assault and battery during a sexual encounter with a woman with whom he had had a 10-year sexual relationship. Albert sought to introduce evidence that his accuser, who had been in a mental hospital six weeks before the alleged assault, had previously made false accusations against men who had left her, as Albert, who was engaged to be married, was planning to do. Albert's offer of proof was denied, compromising his ability to defend himself. Facing a possible life sentence, he chose to plead guilty to misdemeanor assault.

Scapegoating Reasonable Judges

Murphy's dogged attacks on [Judge W. Ferry] Ruckriegle as a veritable "advocate for the accused" are also without foundation. Far from being a black robed patriarch in league with the defendant, Ruckriegle's rulings were reasonable and, if anything, minimalist. It is not the rulings but the reaction to them by victims' advocates and the media which are worrisome.

For example, Ruckriegle granted a defense motion that Bryant's accuser would not be referred to as "the victim" in court. Such labeling, as opposed to "alleged victim" or "accuser," undermines the presumption of innocence. However, this motion was hotly contested by both the prosecution and by victims' rights organizations, which filed amicus briefs and complained that Ruckriegle's decision created an anti-woman double-standard.

Ruckriegle also allowed Bryant to introduce evidence that his accuser had had other sexual encounters in the 72 hours before her medical examination for the alleged assault. Bryant's defense team contended that the microscopic vaginal injuries the prosecution claimed were suffered in the alleged assault could instead have been the product of various consensual sexual encounters.

Media commentators labeled the 72 hour decision a "bombshell for prosecutors" that "threatens all women," and likened Ruckriegle to a man who has "tiptoed into a minefield."

Murphy is correct that rape is a horrible crime. But false accusations of rape are every bit as horrible. They are a form of psychological rape that can emotionally, socially, and economically destroy a person even if there is no conviction, especially for those of less fame and fortune than Bryant. The stigma attaches to the falsely accused for life. Few believe them and few care. Prosecutors systematically refuse to prosecute the perpetrators. And victims' advocates like Murphy refuse to see falsely accused men as victims, and instead work to minimize and conceal the problem.

CHAPTER 2

What Causes Violence Against Women?

Chapter Preface

In order to discover the causes of violence against women, some researchers examine societal attitudes about women and the role of violence in conceptions of masculinity and manhood. Other researchers interview batterers and rapists and use psychological testing to find out why certain individuals become violent. Yet another line of research has emerged in recent decades that examines moments in history when the rate of violence against women has risen dramatically. One important area of study in this research investigates the causes of increased sexual violence against women during times of war. The United Nations calls the sexual violation and torture of women and girls during armed conflict "one of history's great silences."

The lack of concern in past years about wartime violence against women could be due to cultural norms inherited from the Ancient Greek, Roman, and Hebrew civilizations. In all of these societies, it was commonly held that victors in combat deserved the right to "rape and pillage" any villages, kingdoms, or continents they conquered. While it was the dwellings, land, and material riches that were "pillaged," it was women and girls who were raped. Since most of the ancient cultures considered women to be the property of men, the difference between pillaging possessions and raping mothers, daughters, and wives was not considered great.

The practice of raping vanquished women continued into the twentieth century. Some examples include the rape of Jewish women by Cossack soldiers during the Russian pogroms of the early twentieth century; the trafficking of Chinese, Korean, and Philippine "comfort women" by the Japanese military during World War II; the rape of Bengali women by Pakistani soldiers during the 1971 war of succession in Bangladesh; and the use of sexual violence by American GIs in Vietnam to terrorize the population into submission. More recent cases that have achieved some measure of international outrage include the wars in the former Yugoslavia and in Rwanda. Somewhere between 300,000 and 500,000 Tutsi women who survived the genocide in Rwanda were raped. The systematic rape of Bosnian women was a strategy of ethnic cleansing—sometimes to force Bosnian women to flee their country, and at other times to force them to give birth to Serbian babies.

Statistics that show a disturbing rise in sexual violence during times of war have motivated more discussion about what causes whole communities to resort to rape in a specific context and during a particular period of time. Some speculate that the amplified violence can result from a total collapse in the social and moral order that once served to prevent atrocities such as rape in peacetime. The mayhem of fighting simply drives some soldiers into murderous madness. Moreover, women and children are often left without any protection. Nonsoldiers, may also take advantage of the temporary chaos of conflict and commit rape without any fear of retribution.

In other instances, upon the collapse of the former, more compassionate social order, a new social order that condones rape is imposed and severely enforced during war. In her study of the decade-long crackdown against the 1988 democratic uprising in Burma, Betsy Apple analyzes how the new regime successfully imposed an alternate social order on citizens by first ensnaring, debasing, and then brainwashing an army of illiterate, poor, and helpless soldiers. The soldiers, in turn, learned to brutalize citizens into submission. Tellingly, Apple calls the military training of these Tatmadaw soldiers a "school for rape." She links the wide-scale approval of rape as a weapon during the regime to the rigid hierarchy of the army, which encouraged a "credo of domination and violence." She writes:

Ideas about what makes a good warrior help define masculinity in each military context. In the Tatmadaw in particular, power is exerted through violence. Therefore, violence becomes the necessary instrument of all soldiers and officers, and a "good" Tatmadaw soldier or officer is one who is able to both endure and inflict violent abuse. In this way, notions about masculinity, power, and brutal domination become entwined in the Tatmadaw.

The institutional pressures to conform in such circumstances are severe. In order to survive, soldiers adopt the values of the military, eventually believing in and acting out the ideology without remorse. Random cruelty, exploitation, and vicious domination are no longer exceptional. In this kind of social order, raping women and girls simply becomes a part of everyday life.

The variety of viewpoints in this chapter show that there is still much debate about what causes sexual violence against women. However, many who ask what causes the *increase* in sexual violence during times of war agree on one issue. Women are still used as strategic pawns in most efforts to invade, dominate, or decimate villages, nations, and continents of people.

Pornography Contributes to Violence Against Women

John Hughes

John Hughes is editor and chief operating officer of the Deseret Morning News. *He is a former editor of the* Christian Science Monitor.

From his jail cell . . . , 20-year-old Craig Roger Gregerson explained the reason for which he has been arrested and charged with capital murder, punishable by death, and first degree child kidnapping.

In a case that created national media attention, he is accused of killing 5-year-old Destiny Norton, who went missing from her home in Salt Lake City July 16 [2006]. Hundreds turned out to search for her. Later police found her body stuffed in a container in the basement of Gregerson's house just two doors away from her home. Police charge that he lured her to his own property, suffocated her, then abused her dead body.

A Dangerous Addiction

In the jail cell interview with a local TV reporter, Gregerson offered an addiction to pornography as the reason for his actions. When asked why he killed the little girl he said he was "addicted to pornography at one point. It was ruining my life and affecting my relationship with my wife. I can tell you this: I have now become a strong advocate against pornography. I do apologize to the public, and everyone else who's been involved in what happened."

Those who profit from the production and sale of pornographic and violent material in magazines and books, on videos and television, argue that there is no evidence to prove that what they create can foster violence, and child molestation and sex crimes, in those exposed to it.

Judith Reisman, author of The Psychopharmacology of Pictorial Pornography, *sees a direct casual link between pornography and sex crimes.*

The ugly case of Craig Roger Gregerson, and what happened to 5-year-old Destiny Norton, is at least one convincing piece of evidence that it can and does.

Society Is Easily Influenced

It should not require a doctorate in psychology to understand that what we see and hear can influence our behavior.

But if evidence is needed, there is serious research that proves this to be the case. For instance, the Rand Corporation in Pittsburgh has just published in the current issue of *Pediatrics* the results of a survey indicating that teens who listen to music full of raunchy, sexual lyrics start having sex sooner than those who prefer other songs. The *Associated Press* quotes the lead researcher on this project, Steven Martino, as saying: Exposure to lots of sexually degrading music "gives them a specific message about sex." Boys learn they should be relentless in pursuit of women, and girls learn to view themselves as sex objects. "We think that really lowers kids' inhibitions."

Benjamin Chavis, who heads a network coalition of hiphop musicians and recording industry executives, responded to the survey by asserting that explicit music lyrics are a cultural expression that reflect "social and economic realities."

This is a familiar echo of the plaint by some Hollywood movie and TV producers who argue that when they splatter their movies and TV productions with violence, profanity and lurid sexuality, they are merely reflecting society as it is. To be asked to clean up their acts is an infringement upon their artistic freedom, they say.

A Casual Link Between Pornography and Sex Crimes

Nobody suggests that everybody addicted to pornography becomes a violent person or sexual predator. But as Corydon Hammon, co-director of the Sex and Marital Therapy Clinic at the University of Utah says, "I don't think I've ever yet seen an adult sex offender who was not involved with pornography." Judith Reisman, author of *The Psychopharmacology of Pictorial Pornography*, sees a direct casual link between pornography and sex crimes. "In many cases I don't think we have any problem saying pornography caused (the sex offense). We have tons of data."

Free Speech

Congress has attempted legislation seeking to control pornography but found it vetoed by courts claiming the legislation hobbled free speech. The courts, on the same free speech ground, have outlawed the sale of videos in which commercial companies have edited out profanity or questionable scenes.

A new legislative attempt may require cable TV channels, where most questionable material appears, to carry a label warning of the offensiveness but without deleting it, thus circumventing the free speech issue.

Pornography Is a Drug

The Kaiser Foundation has undertaken extensive research on the amount of sex-oriented and violent programming on TV and its impact on young viewers.

The watchdog group Parents Television Council has campaigned vigorously against sex, violence and profanity on television and in other media. It has lobbied against the cable industry's mandatory inclusion of questionable channels in omnibus packages offered subscribers, arguing that subscribers should have the right to pick and choose individual channels.

Human sexuality researcher Reisman gets it right when she says: "It's not that pornography acts like a drug. It is a drug."

Pornography Does Not Cause Violence Against Women

Paul Nathanson and Katherine K. Young

Paul Nathanson and Katherine K. Young are faculty members in the Department of Religious Studies at McGill University in Montreal, Canada.

There are some good reasons for tolerating pornography and prostitution, which is not to say that there are good reasons for celebrating either.

Human existence would surely be easier if people had no need for sex apart from procreation. Maybe it would be easier if only we could control that need more effectively than we have. But would we be happier? To answer that question, think about the quality of life in societies that make the most intense efforts to control or deny human nature: totalitarian ones. Even if these societies could make people happier, which they do not, they would still be likely to fail in the long run. Tightly controlled societies endure only as long as conditions remain stable, as they do in relatively isolated societies (although even these, according to the current generation of anthropologists, are never either completely isolated or completely static) but not in modern ones. Because they discourage innovation, the basic requirement for which is freedom of thought and the basic training for which is freedom to play, societies that depend very heavily on orthodoxy and conformity discourage the kind of adaptability required to face change effectively. The most obvious example of inflexibility in recent times, of course, is that of Eastern Europe under communism. But another example, the one that is most prevalent here and now, is surely the mentality inherent in ideological feminism.

Like communism, ideological feminism is utopian. Ignoring the ambiguity and ambivalence that have always characterized human existence, it directly or indirectly proclaims that society would be happy if only it was more thoroughly controlled by the state. In other words, it focuses attention heavily on power, believing that women have less power than men (which is true in some ways though not others) but also believing that power itself should be the primary factor in creating a new and presumably better society. For women to prosper, in other words, they must control men by wielding more power over them (even though Marilyn French and some other ideological feminists assert that "power over" is a distinctively "male" preoccupation). . . .

Eliminate Double Standards

At the very least, we should acknowledge the need for a single moral standard and a single legal one. If porn is bad because it dehumanizes women, it is surely just as bad because it dehumanizes men (either those men who are depicted in porn or those who use it). And if it is bad for men to create or buy porn, then it is surely bad for women to do the same thing. But how many women actually use porn? Very few, if you confine your inquiry to the most obvious equivalents. (At least some readers of *Playgirl*, in fact, are probably gay men.) Very many, on the other hand, if you consider various functional equivalents.

It would seem that (straight) men have only "one thing" on their minds: not merely having sex with women, but having sex with unwilling *women.*

In *Spreading Misandry*, we discussed the dehumanization of men in popular culture, especially in movies and on television shows. Think now about romance novels, which are written by and for women. In these books—sold at every supermarket, this formulaic genre is probably more lucrative than any other—men are reduced to the wealthy fantasy objects of female protagonists. Consider also "women's magazines" and "teen 'zines." In these publications, women or girls learn how to "catch" and "hold" men or boys. They do not present readers with coarse or vulgar pictures, to be sure, but they do encourage readers to objectify, and even manipulate the opposite sex. And what about soap operas? These shows manage to objectify both sexes, actually, because both are presented as sexually and financially predatory.

By far the most disturbing venue for objectifying and even dehumanizing men, though, would be the books and articles written by feminist ideologues. These publications encourage readers—either overtly or covertly, directly or indirectly—to feel contempt for men as inferior beings or even to hate men as the source of all suffering and evil throughout history. The usual justification is based on the assumption that men have such godlike power that nothing can damage them. This, we believe, is a false and dangerous assumption. It implies that women are justified in using any means short of violence . . . to promote a social, economic, and legal revolution. Classic (but by no means rare) examples would include the following feminists: Robin Morgan, author of *Demon Lover*; Marilyn French, author of *Beyond Power* (a massive compendium purporting to show not only that men are both evil and inferior to women but that so is maleness itself in just about every species) and *The War against Women*; Andrea Dworkin, author of *Intercourse*; and Catharine MacKinnon, author of *Toward a Feminist Theory of the State*. The list could go on and on. These authors implicitly deny the full humanity of male people.

The fact that some of these authors—not all but some—stop short of basing their claims on maleness itself does not make the sinister creatures that they describe recognizable as real human beings. They are not the complex, ambivalent, and confused people who actually co-exist in daily life with equally complex, ambivalent, and confused women (much less those who actually live with women in imperfect but mutually sustaining relationships). From what these authors say, it would seem that (straight) men have only "one thing" on their minds: not merely having sex with women but having sex with *unwilling* women—or, failing that, using some other, closely related way of subjugating women. . . .

One might ask feminists who want to ban porn why they do not want to ban television as well?

Every society should acknowledge, and most do, that not everyone is going to marry and that trying to impose life-long asceticism on people who do not is unfair. In any case, if pornography and prostitution are made illegal, many people will meet their needs illegally and often in ways that are dangerous for society. Since some people will disobey the law no matter what, that argument does not in itself provide a good enough reason to legalize their behaviour, but it does provide a good enough reason to weigh the pros and cons very carefully. . . .

Violent Fantasy Is Not Reality

We have argued that there are some good reasons for tolerating both pornography and prostitution. But not in all contexts. We refer specifically to contexts involving violence and minors. Some have seen them at one time or another, pictures of people choking partners during oral sex or of torturing them for erotic pleasure. Others have even experienced acts of this kind with prostitutes. Maybe these are not just innocent fantasies; maybe they reveal at least the secret desire to inflict pain. Maybe, though not necessarily. They might in fact be merely fantasies, daydreams that explore the forbidden. As a form of play, porn can be linked with both anarchy or violence and artistic or intellectual creativity. The link is inconvenient, to be sure, but not necessarily evil. The case against "rough sex" or sado-masochism can be made effectively, but it is more complicated than meets the eye.

Here is an analogous situation: the imaginative exploration of murder in mainstream movies. Everyone recognizes that these movies are fictional. Moreover, they are placed within a moral framework. Until the day before yesterday, as it were, moviegoers were always expected to believe that murder is indeed evil and that those who do evil will be brought to justice. But critics of violent porn might say that because it is more or less hidden from view, it lacks that moral framework. Its defenders might reply that it allows people to explore fantasies that have nothing to do with the real world, ones that they would never act out in real life. And they might add that the moral framework is sometimes very ambiguous in mainstream movies, particularly in some recent ones, but also even in earlier ones. You have only to think of one famous scene in *Gone with the Wind*. Rhett carries Scarlett, against her will, up to the bedroom and has "his way" with her. Next morning, however, a delighted Scarlett wants more of the same from Rhett. Well, was she raped or not? And if so, are viewers— female viewers—justified in enjoying the fantasy? Should this movie be banned or the scene excised by censors?

We see no reason to oppose the production of erotic imagery.

A similar question arises with respect to violence on television. It is true that a few viewers go out and copy the violence they see on television, and there is some evidence that children and adolescents who watch a lot of violent shows are more likely than others to become violent in the future. But most viewers, by far, do nothing of the kind. Clearly, then, some *additional* factor or factors must be involved in cases of antisocial behaviour. If additional factors were not involved, one might ask feminists who want to ban porn why they do not want to ban television as well? And if not all forms of television, why not at least some forms? Possibly because feminists present porn as a threat to women alone (despite gay porn), which makes it easy for them to conceptualize porn as a "women's issue." They can hardly say the same of violence on television, which presents at least as many male victims of violence as female ones. But if violence against women is intolerable, why not violence against men as well? Is the latter acceptable merely because in many cases both the culprits and the victims are men, as if the victims somehow deserve their fate by virtue of their common maleness?

Censorship Is Not the Answer

The problem of ambiguity aside, would women actually be safer if men were denied outlets such as porn or prostitution? Who knows? In the papers collected for *In Harm's Way*, McKinnon and Dworkin, along with many others, present evidence of porn leading directly to violence against women, although they say little or nothing about gay porn leading to violence against men or even about lesbian porn leading to violence against women.

Can pornography and prostitution lead to violence? Of course they can. Must they do so? Are they inherently evil? Not unless human nature itself—and, in this context, most people would think of male human nature—is evil. Here is the implicit deductive argument that underlies this entire discussion: All men like porn; porn is evil; all those who like something that is evil are themselves evil; ergo, all men are evil. There are those who believe precisely this. When people discuss porn in the public square (and even within religious communities, which often agree with radical feminism on that particular topic), they should at least acknowledge one of the several things at stake: the condemnation of an entire group of people on biological grounds.

But something must still be done about pornography and prostitution (although minors are already protected). Like so many other unregulated or deregulated industries, they can cause serious harm. Apart from any ways in which they endanger women in particular, after all, they are currently operating in ways that endanger society as a whole. Partly because of their marginal status as underground operations, for instance, both are heavily associated with drugs and violence. The solution most commonly proposed by ideological feminists in the United States and Canada is to ban them, or at least try to do so. At stake in that solution, especially in connection with porn, is freedom of expression, which raises several questions. Is society more in danger from the absence of freedom or the misuse of freedom? Is society more in danger from conformity or nonconformity? We suggest that no solution will work unless it accepts ambiguity and therefore compromise. From this point of view, it would make sense for the law to presume that people are free to conduct their lives as they see fit but also to limit that freedom—and freedom is always limited to activities that do not endanger others—when either violence or minors are involved.

Many who turn to either pornographic images or prostitutes are unable to find sexual gratification in more satisfying ways.

What, then, would we actually suggest in the way of law reform? As for pornography, we see no reason to oppose the production of erotic imagery. On the other hand, we support the current prohibition of material that either depicts or involves minors in its production. In addition, we would encourage legislation against violent porn but not against vague ideas of the "subordination of women." And as for prostitution, we see no reason to oppose payment for sexual services.

To put it bluntly, we would stop the prosecution, even persecution, not only of adult prostitutes but also of their adult customers.

Porn Serves a Purpose

Although some erotic pornography is classified as art and although high-end prostitutes live and work in very comfortable conditions, pornography and prostitution are heavily associated with the lurid and the sordid. Why tolerate these industries? Because, whether some people want to admit it or not, both pornography and prostitution serve a very widespread need. And not only for men. As Frederick Mathews points out in connection with a study by the National Juvenile Prostitution Survey, half the juvenile prostitutes reported that they had been approached by female customers or female pimps, or "procuresses." Of these prostitutes, 62% were male and 43.4% females. Women do enjoy watching the Chippendales [male strippers] "dance," watching steamy soap operas, and reading romance novels. And all those things are forms of porn, albeit ones that most people consider respectable.

Many who turn to either pornographic images or prostitutes are unable to find sexual gratification in more satisfying ways—that is, in the context of marriage or some other durable relationship, rather than in the context of a business transaction. These people lack the money, good looks, personality skills, or whatever, to attract spouses. And far from being an inherent threat to marriage, as we say, pornographic images and prostitutes might actually prevent at least a few marriages from disintegrating due to affairs; people pay for them, after all, without loving them. Those involved in these industries—male or female, gay or straight—would become providers of a service like any other. Not love, which cannot be hired, but sex. This is particularly important in the case of prostitutes. In a regulated industry—and prostitution is regulated in some European countries—they could participate in the economy: paying taxes but also collecting sickness or un-employment insurance, old-age pensions, and so on. Govern-ment inspection or supervision, moreover, could provide them with healthier working conditions and eliminate pimps. . . .

Don't Scapegoat Porn

If we ban violent pornography for leading to violence against women in real life, for instance, then we should ban violent popular culture as well—that would include movies, songs, and even some segments of news shows—for leading to vio-lence against everyone. If we ban it for expressing hatred against women, then we should ban feminist books and other productions that express hatred against men. If we ban merely erotic porn for objectifying women, then we should ban ro-mance novels, along with ideological diatribes for "objectify-ing" men.

Men Are Biologically Inclined to Rape

John Alcock

John Alcock is a professor in the school of life sciences at Arizona State University in Tempe and the author of many publications about sociobiology.

The idea that sexual motivation plays *no* part in rape seems decidedly counterintuitive, given that the vast majority of rapists are sufficiently sexually aroused to achieve an erection and to ejaculate in their victims. Yet many persons have no doubt about it; sexual desire is not an issue in the rapist's behavior. The appeal of this assertion must stem from the fact that most people consider sexual desire a "natural" phenomenon, which some feminists fear will make the public more willing to excuse the rapist, at least in part, on the grounds that rape is in some sense "natural." In contrast, if rape is said to be violence pure and simple driven by a criminal desire to brutalize and humiliate, then no one would be tempted to forgive the rapist or be more understanding of his behavior. In other words, acceptance of the naturalistic fallacy provides the impetus to insist that there is nothing "natural" about the causes of rape.

To this end, it is also valuable to claim that rape is a purely human phenomenon, not part of the sexuality of other species. . . . Moreover, why not assert that rape is a purely cultural phenomenon, the invention of some men in some warped societies. If true, then one need "only" educate the members of that society in order to change the ruling male ideology of rape, which will eliminate the problem. To this end, many feminists assert that rape is not a universal feature of all societies but rather a manifestation of just those societies in which a particularly unfortunate ideological perspective has come to shape male attitudes and behavior.

Rape and Fear

The advocates of the "rape has nothing to do with sex" hypothesis have been circumspect in dealing with the relevant data. For example, with respect to the so-called uniqueness of rape, even when [Susan] Brownmiller wrote her book [*Against Our Will*] in 1975, ample evidence existed that males from a very wide range of animals sometimes force themselves on females that struggle to prevent copulation from occurring. Over the years, much more information has been assembled on the practice of forced matings in everything from insects to chimpanzees, orangutans, and other primate relatives of man. . . .

And what about the claim that rape is haphazardly distributed among human cultures, present here, absent there, thanks to arbitrary variation in cultural histories and influences? You will remember [anthropologist] Margaret Mead's incorrect assertion that rape was absent in traditional Samoan society. Analysis of similar claims about other groups has shown them to be equally erroneous. Rape is a cultural universal.

These findings are part of the reason why some sociobiologists think that the "rape has nothing to do with sex" hypothesis is not only implausible but untrue. One sociobiological alternative is that rape is partly the product of evolved male psychological mechanisms, including those that promote ease of sexual arousal, the capacity for impersonal sex, the desire for sexual variety for variety's sake, a desire to control the sexuality of potential partners, and a willingness to employ coercive tactics to achieve copulations under some conditions. Why would these proximate mechanisms have spread through ancestral hominid populations? Because they almost certainly contributed to an increase in the number of females inseminated by some ancestral males with a consequent increase in the number of offspring produced. . . .

Male psychological mechanisms make it easy for the sexually coercive male to justify his actions and to overlook the great emotional damage that his behavior causes women.

What are the implications of these findings for persons who want to reduce the frequency of rape by educating potential rapists? The rape-is-not-sex theorists would have us tell these individuals that rape occurs strictly as a result of a male desire to dominate and humiliate women. The logic of this argument dictates that as long as a man felt sexual desire while interacting with a woman, then he could convince himself (falsely) that whatever he did could not constitute rape. I do not believe that this outcome is desirable, nor is it helpful to those who would like to make rape less common in human societies. . . .

Bad for Society

The eagerness of the critics to marginalize the evolutionary approach to rape and to disparage those with whom they disagree presumably arises from their belief that it would be bad for society to entertain the possibility of an evolutionary theory of rape. Far better, according to these persons, to stick to such notions as "rape is not about sex" and "all rapists are criminally violent individuals." [Jerry] Coyne, for one, appears to acknowledge that these assertions are not necessarily true, but he lets the matter slide: "one must remember that they originated not as scientific propositions but as political slogans deemed necessary to reverse popular misconceptions about rape."

But is it a good idea to base a desirable social goal—a reduction in rape—on a scientifically indefensible claim? Steven

Pinker does not think so: "It is a bad idea to say that war, violence, rape, and greed are bad because humans are not naturally inclined to them." And I agree with Pinker because, as he points out, such a proposition implies that (1) any number of highly undesirable human behaviors would have to be accepted if it were shown that they were natural in the sense of having an evolved basis or that (2) evolutionary scientists should conceal or misrepresent their findings.

Humans are not robots whose every action advances the welfare of our genes.

But what if evolutionary data, rather than ideological strategy, were used to develop a high school rape prevention program (yes, I know the certain response of a school board to such a program, but permit me to dream on). My course would instruct young men that past selection has burdened them with a genetic heritage which made it probable they would develop a certain kind of sexual psychology, one that may have promoted reproductive success in the past but one that can also have various unfortunate consequences in the present, some of them sure to be judged immoral or illegal. In particular, the great interest in sexual relations and extreme ease of sexual arousal that made our male ancestors less likely to miss opportunities to copulate and have children can lead some men today to engage in a spectrum of coercive activities, ranging from pleading for sex with potential partners, to subjecting dates to unpleasant psychological pressure, to employing mild physical force with female companions leading to date rape, to the violent sexual assault of women known or unknown to the rapists, some of whom may indeed be genuine psychopaths. My sociobiologically based education program would also explain why male psychological mechanisms make it easy for the sexually coercive male to justify his actions and to overlook the great emotional damage that his behavior causes women.

Dealing with the Truth

The ultimate reason why women find behavior that thwarts freedom of mate choice so distressing and devastating would be placed on the table in front of those attending my socio-biological sex education class. In the past, rape almost certainly imposed a major fitness cost on women, and the same is generally true in the present. As noted, raped women sometimes do become pregnant, which may cause current husbands to abandon them rather than care for a child fathered by another male. Even if the raped woman avoids producing a child by the rapist, the event, if known to a husband, may actually generate hostility rather than sympathy, such is the nature of the evolved male brain, with its adaptive but cruelly paranoid tendencies when it comes to the risk of caring for offspring other than one's own. Given the damaging fitness consequences of being raped, selection has favored women in the past who did their very best to avoid this fate. One product of selection of this sort has been the psychological mechanisms that generate emotional pain when rape occurs. Such psychological systems may motivate the raped woman to avoid the situation that resulted in her victimization; more importantly, the extreme distress of the rape victim may also communicate convincingly to her social partner, if she has one, that she truly was a victim and in no way cooperated with the rapist.

With these basics in mind, our now partially educated young men would be informed that they need not permit their evolved psyches, which are after all working on behalf of their genes, to lead them into actions that could cause others such unhappiness. They must realize that the male drive to have sex will often greatly exceed that of their female companions. Moreover, their eagerness can cause them to misinterpret the intentions of others, to take a smile or a friendly comment as a signal of sexual receptivity when this may be the last thing on the woman's mind. Since they now understand these things, they can be on guard against the pernicious effects of past natural selection, an unfeeling process with some exceedingly unpleasant effects, which everyone needs to know about.

Moreover, our now somewhat more evolutionarily conscious young men could be told that there is no reason they cannot overcome certain damaging psychological predispositions that selection has favored. In fact, every day people all over the globe defeat the ultimate "wishes" of their naturally selected genes because natural selection has also given us a modicum of rationality. I speak from some personal experience here. Although my brain has been designed by selection to motivate me to do that which would result in having as many surviving offspring as possible (at least in the ancestral environment of humans); I have not let evolution push me around. My wife and I made the decision to have only two children, although we almost certainly could have had more. In employing a vasectomy as a means of achieving reproductive restraint, I am not alone.

That humans are not robots whose every action advances the welfare of our genes stems from several factors. . . . Our genes' survival is dependent upon proximate mechanisms that motivate us to do things which were only correlated with gene propagation in the past, and never perfectly correlated. Our genes do not control us directly but instead influence the development of psychological mechanisms that typically operate with rules of thumb that usually, but not always, generate adaptive responses in certain environments. We have, moreover, changed the human environment from its ancestral condition in part because of the technological spinoffs from scientific discoveries that were made thanks to certain evolved features of our brains. As a result, our decision-making rules of thumb now express themselves in an environment far different from the ancestral one, which makes it less likely that our actions will benefit our genes. I could therefore hope to change the behavior of the young men in my sociobiological sex education class by providing them information unknown to their ancestors. I would suggest to them, "You can combat the dictatorship of your evolved psyches. The next time your hormones take over, remember that you can behave adaptively in evolutionary terms, in other words, often like a bozo or worse, or you can fight those evolved impulses when they threaten to damage someone else, a result that has grave consequences for your own welfare as well." I would point out to my class that having been educated, they could no longer use ignorance as an excuse, should they choose to engage in sexually coercive behavior of any sort.

Having seen [actor] John Cleese (in the highly philosophical movie *The Meaning of Life*) fail miserably when he tried to teach the finer points of sexual intercourse by example to a class of young men, despite his best efforts and those of his partner, I doubt that a sociobiological version of a sex education class would dramatically alter the behavior of the adolescents in the course. But it might be worth a try.

If given the chance, I would also have a go at educating young women as well. I'd tell young women, as well as young men, that evolutionary theory is worth knowing about because it helps to have an accurate understanding of human nature. I'd also point out that because the fitness interests of the two sexes are not identical, and sometimes are in direct conflict, male and female sexual psychologies are not the same. And I'd tell the women an anecdote that provides a sobering view of the enormity of the difference. One of the major supermarket chains instructed its checkout workers, generally women, to look the customer in the eye and smile when handing over the receipt and change, while saying, "Thanks Mr. (or Mrs.) X for shopping at Safeway." Female employees soon petitioned management to please let them skip the eye-contact-with-smile routine because so many men instantly interpreted their behavior as a come-on of some sort, which led them to make "reciprocal" sexual invitations to the checkout clerks. Which tells you something about men, namely, that they almost always view women of reproductive age as potential sex objects (no matter what they say in the interest of political correctness or a desire to deceive women or to ingratiate themselves with possible sexual partners). It cannot hurt to know this fact of life, and a few others, such as the willingness of even nice guys to resort to coercive tactics to secure sex. As Robert Wright has pointed out, women really should take the time to Know the Enemy.

I am not kidding myself that schools in North America will soon be clamoring for evolutionarily informed sex education classes nor do I believe that an understanding of natural selection would usher in a golden age of societal tranquility. But at the very least, if people really did understand what evolutionary theory was all about, perhaps they would know that "natural" or "evolved" traits were neither inevitable nor necessarily desirable from a personal or societal perspective. No one is under obligation to accept our evolved attributes as moral necessities. As the evolutionary biologist Richard Dawkins says, "My own philosophy of life begins with an explicit rejection of Darwinism as a normative principle for living, even while I extol it as the explanatory principle for life."

The great evolutionist George C. Williams is even more emphatic: "With what other than condemnation is a person with any moral sense to respond to a system in which the ultimate purpose in life is to be better than your neighbor at getting genes into future generations." As Williams points out, those parasitic organisms that cause disease are beautifully adapted in ways that benefit their genes while causing immense distress and pain in their victims. The fact that interactions among the members of the same species are also guided by adaptations of various sorts is no guarantee of happiness and harmony, as dysfunctional step-families and couples in sexual conflict demonstrate all too clearly. If more people realized how our naturally selected brain acts in the service of our genes, then perhaps they would be less inclined to endure the consequences of natural selection, a blind process that cares not a whit about human beings or anything else.

Claims that Men Are Biologically Inclined to Rape Are Faulty

Michael Kimmel

Michael Kimmel is a sociologist and author of numerous books about feminism, men, and masculinity, including Men Confront Pornography *and* Against the Tide: Pro-Feminist Men in the United States, 1776–1990.

It was while watching my 22-month-old son playing with our neighbor's daughter the other day that I was convinced to respond in some way to the view [Randy] Thornhill and [Craig] Palmer [authors of *A Natural History of Rape*] have of my little boy, and their view of his future—a future of unbridled sexual predation, of the evolutionary justification for using any means necessary—fraud or force, drugs or alcohol—to sexually conquer an unwilling female (or male, but Thornhill and Palmer think other males would be more compliant). And the life of our little neighbor is even more bleak: She will have to be constantly on her guard because boys will be boys—which is to say that boys will be violent little rapacious predatory beasts. She will have to modify her behavior, watch what she wears, where she walks, and at what time, because there's certainly no way we're going to be able to protect her from those little male monsters.

I see a different reality, and I want a different future for my children than that which Thornhill and Palmer lay out for them. Fortunately, in the real world, in which I happen to live, Thornhill and Palmer's prognosis is merely political resignation with a pseudo-scientific facade. My son will live in a different world, because he already does, because the real world he and I live in bears little resemblance to the world Thornhill and Palmer describe, and because works like Thornhill and Palmer's, however politically resigned they are, offer no real vision and no real hope.

And no real science either. I will argue that this "natural history" contains dreadfully poor understanding of nature, of history, and of "natural history." The book tells us less about "the biological bases of sexual coercion" than the ideological fantasies of those who justify sexual coercion. It's bad science, bad history, and bad politics—or, more accurately, it's bad politics masquerading as science. . . .

Bad Science

Evolutionary psychology is a social science, which is to say it is an oxymoron. It cannot conform to the canons of a science like physics, in which falsifiability is its chief goal and replication its chief method. It does not account for variations in its universalizing pronouncements, nor does it offer the most parsimonious explanations. It is speculative theory, often provocative and interesting, but no more than that. It is like—gasp!—my own discipline of sociology. And, like sociology, there are some practitioners who will do virtually anything to be taken seriously as "science," despite the fact that individual human beings happily confound all predictions based on aggregate models of behavior.

Telling us that it [rape] is natural tells us nothing about it except that it is found in nature.

Typically, to stake its claim for legitimacy, pseudo-science cloaks itself in vociferous denunciations of all other pseudo-sciences. In this case, Thornhill and Palmer set up straw man arguments, attribute them to a social science utterly in the thrall of feminist rape hysteria, and then claim to demolish them with pseudo-scientific assertions based on selective evidence. No wonder one medical reviewer noted the irony "that a book purporting such devotion to science should have so little in it" and evolutionary biologist Jerry Coyne calls the work "utterly lacking in sound scientific grounding," "an embarrassment to the field," and "useless and unscientific."

The "argument" of the book is actually a tautology. Rape, they claim, is "a natural, biological phenomenon that is a product of human evolutionary heritage." Well, of course it is. As is *any* behavior or trait found among human primates. If it exists in nature, it's natural. Some "natural" beverages contain artificial—"social"—additives that give them their color, their texture, their taste, their "meaning" or "significance." This is equally true of rape. Telling us that it is natural tells us nothing about it except that it is found in nature. . . .

Evolutionary Theory About Gender

Proof of this argument is based first on Robert Trivers's reductionist evolutionary theory, which suggests that males and females have different reproductive strategies based on the size and number of their reproductive cells. From sperm and egg we get motivation, intention, perhaps even cognition. Male reproductive success comes from impregnating as many females as possible; females' success comes from enticing a male to provide and protect the vulnerable and dependent offspring. Thus males have a natural predisposition toward promiscuity, sex without love, and parental indifference; females have a natural propensity for monogamy, love as a precondition of sex, and parental involvement.

Rape may also be about sexual repulsion, about rage and fear, about domination.

This arrangement gives women a lot of power. Since males are more eager for sex than females, this gives females the power to choose which males are going to be successful.

Thornhill and Palmer offer rape as the evolutionary mating strategy of losers, males who cannot otherwise get a date. "But getting chosen is not the only way to gain sexual access to females," they write. "In rape, the male circumvents the females' choice."

Trivers's arguments have been effectively refuted by primatologist Sarah Blaffer Hrdy, who has used the same empirical observations to construct an equally plausible case for females' natural propensity toward promiscuity (to seduce many males into believing the offspring is theirs and thus ensure survival by increasing food and protection from those males) and males' natural propensity toward monogamy (to avoid being run ragged providing for offspring that may—or may not—be their own).

Some Bad Assumptions

Thornhill and Palmer's use of Trivers's speculations makes two assumptions about rape and sex. First, they assume that rape is only about sex. "Rapists are sexually motivated," they write. Second, they assume that sex is only about reproduction. Neither of these is supported by the evidence.

To be sure, as Thornhill and Palmer note, rape *can be* about sex. Surely, three decades of feminist advocacy and social science research on date and acquaintance rape indicates that some rapes are a product of a combination of sexual desire, contempt for women's bodily integrity, and a feeling of sexual entitlement. (Ironically, Thornhill and Palmer's thesis works better for date and acquaintance rape than it does for stranger rape, which is their model. After all, at least some modicum of desire is potentially present.) There are few, if any, feminists or social scientists who would, today, argue that rape is *never* about sex.

But if rape can sometimes also be partly about sex, it is not *only* about sex. Gang rape, prison rape, military rape of entire subject populations, rape prior to murder, rape *after* murder—these don't necessarily admit to rape-as-alternate-strategy-to-express-sexual-desire. Rape may also be about sexual repulsion, about rage and fear, about domination. Rape of women may be a homosocial event, by which one group of men expresses its domination over another group of men. Rape is a multidimensional phenomenon, offering a large amount of variation. Thornhill and Palmer's view of rape is monochromatic and embraces only a small fraction of its remarkable variety.

Those countries in which women hold more political offices, in which women equal men in the professions, in which there is adequate sex education—all have lower rape rates than we do.

Men use their penises for many motivations, and they aren't all necessarily reproductive. Sex can be about play, about pleasure, about cementing bonds between females and males, or between males or between females. It may—or it may not—have anything to do with reproduction. (I would bet that neither Thornhill nor Palmer has more than three children each, and that both have made love more than three times. I hope that their partners would tell a story of two men who know sex is not only about reproduction.) The clitoris, for example, seems to have evolved strictly because of its capacity for pleasure. Since it evolved, then, it means that women's pleasure has something to do with reproductive success in humans. . . .

Bad History

Thornhill and Palmer's bad science is complemented by equally bad history. It's hard to explain the persistence of rape in modern society, except as some unnecessary evolutionary residue like the appendix or tonsils. But they compound this by arguing against all their own evidence that rape is more prevalent today than ever before.

Rape rates in modern society are so high because "in such societies women rarely are chaperoned and often encounter social circumstances that make them vulnerable to rape." More: "The common practice of unsupervised dating in cars and private homes, which is often accompanied by the consumption of alcohol, has placed young women in environments that are conducive to rape to an extent that is probably unparalleled in history."

I would hypothesize precisely the opposite, that rape rates are lower today than ever before. Rape was *far* more likely in medieval Europe, for example. It's just that we called it something else. Ever hear of "right of first night"? (That's coerced sex without consent, that is, rape.) In many societies, rape was a common and legitimate punishment for all sorts of perceived crimes against men. And it is *by far* safer to be a woman alone walking on the street at night today in a modern society than it has ever been. (This is decidedly *not* to say it is safe— just safer.)

Rape Is Reduced by Greater Respect for Women

I believe that rape rates are lower today because women have more power, including the power to redefine behavior that was once seen as normative sexual "etiquette" as date rape. In my high school locker room, I was counseled by older athletes that "it doesn't count unless you put it in." I was advised to "keep going, even if she says no, even if she screams, even if she pushes you away. Don't stop until she hits you," was the felicitous way they put it. (Incidentally, when I mentioned this to my students a few weeks ago, one of the men said, sardonically, "You stopped too soon, man. It's 'don't stop until she *hurts* you.'")

If we were honest about it, then, men of my generation (I'm 50) would have to confess that virtually all of us are "failed attempted date rapists." What we called "dating" is now against the law. (Yes, of course, some were successful. But my point is that the norms have changed, and that such behavior is increasingly problematized, thus making dating safer for women than ever.)

Comparatively, rape rates vary enormously among cultures. And the best variable that determines those rape rates is women's status. Those countries in which women's wages come closer to matching men's (so the men won't feel they are owed something after spending money on their date) have rape rates lower than ours. Those countries in which women hold more political offices, in which women equal men in the professions, in which there is adequate sex education—all have lower rape rates than we do.

Feminists . . . believe that men are capable of doing better, of stopping rape and expressing an equally evolutionarily ordained imperative toward pleasure, mutuality, and equality.

Bad Politics

Lowering rape rates is a political discussion, a discussion about the effectiveness of specific policy proposals. And here Thornhill and Palmer's bad history leads inevitably to bad politics. They make two policy recommendations that they believe will reduce the scourge of rape. The first is transparently silly because it blames the victim. Women must be informed about men's biological predisposition to rape because it *does* matter how they dress and which parties they choose to go to. The best our authors can offer is that women should be warned about how predatory men are. After that, well, they're on their own. (It's a good idea to give them that warning when they get their driver's licenses, since they will need their cars to escape men's violent predations. But, of course, Thornhill and Palmer actually want to use driver's licenses to warn *men* of their own base proclivities.)

The press release that accompanied my copy of the book notes that the authors recommend that "young women consider the biological causes of rape when making decisions about dress, appearance, and social activities." "But where is the evidence that women in mini-skirts are more likely to be raped than women in dirndls [dresses with full skirts]?" asks Barbara Ehrenreich. "Women were raped by the thousands in Bosnia for example, and few if any of them were wearing bikinis or bustiers." Many rapes—in war, in prison—have nothing to do with ensuring reproductive success and everything to do with domination and humiliation of other men. Rape may be far more of a homosocial act than a heterosexual one.

Hatred of Men

The second policy recommendation—about males—reveals Thornhill and Palmer's real political agenda—and it is not a pretty picture. You see, Thornhill and Palmer hate men.

Rarely, if ever, have I read a book that is so resolutely and relentlessly anti-male. *A Natural History of Rape* is the best example I can find of male-bashing masquerading as academic pseudo-science. In their eyes, all men are violent, rapacious predators, seeking to spew their sperm far and wide, at whatever creature happens in their testosterone-crazed evolutionary path. Oh, sure, they try and sugarcoat it:

> human males in all societies so far examined in the ethnographic record possess genes that can lead, by way of ontogeny, to raping behavior when the necessary environmental factors are present, and ... the necessary environmental factors are sometimes present in all societies studied to date.

So all men have the genetic "motivation" to rape and all they need is a social permission.

Wait a minute? Isn't that what they claim the feminists they are trying to discredit argued also? Is that not the justification for zero-tolerance for rape? Isn't that the justification for sensible arguments, like those of Peggy Reeves Sanday, to reduce risk of rape by increasing women's status?

As a policy recommendation, Thornhill and Palmer propose that we institute "an evolutionarily informed education program for young men that focuses on increasing their ability to restrain their sexual behavior."

"Restrain"? Is it that bad? How about "express"—their equally evolution-based biological drive to experience pleasure, mutuality, and fun? Might we not be "hard wired" for that as well? Education for restraint is perhaps the second most politically bankrupt policy initiative around, and utterly ineffective. (The first is demanding that women "just say no.") If Thornhill and Palmer were right—and of course they are not—then the only sensible solution would be to lock all males up and release them for sporadic, reproductive mating after being chosen by females.

The Hope of Feminism

Thornhill and Palmer offer a far more "misandrous" account of rape than anything offered by their nemeses, radical feminists. In the process, they do an enormous disservice to thinking about rape, and, ironically, they end up reproducing the very canards about men that they project onto feminist women. Feminists, by contrast, believe that men are capable of doing better, of stopping rape and expressing an equally evolutionarily ordained imperative toward pleasure, mutuality, and equality.

Bad science, bad history, and bad politics add up to a pretty dreadful book. What's missing, ultimately, from Thornhill and Palmer's facile reductionism is the distinctly human capacity for change, for choice. What's missing is human agency.

To them, men are driven by evolutionary imperatives to rape, pillage, destroy to make sure our seed gets planted. If women are not compliant, we men are hard wired to take what we want anyway. They have the power of choice, but when we're not chosen—well, we get testy. "They made us do it because we can't get them any other way. And we simply *must* have them."

Sexism Causes Violence Against Women

Brian Nichols

Brian Nichols is the public policy team manager for Men Stopping Violence, a national organization that works to end men's violence against women.

As programs for batterers proliferate around the country, they often become a touchstone for disagreements over the source of battering. Is battering a psychological problem, an anger management problem, a communication problem? How a community understands the source of battering in many ways determines the type of program it will support.

In considering the source of battering, it may be helpful to take a look at Bill, a man who batters and is in a batterers intervention program. Bill has acknowledged using force against his partner, Janet; isolating her by blocking the doorway when she wants to leave, criticizing her friends, taking her keys, unplugging the phone, and staying out without telling her where he is. How do we understand his violence, and how does Bill go about making personal change? How these questions are answered has meaning and consequences for the community.

Common Explanations of Battering

Battering has come to be commonly understood as a learned behavior, especially likely to occur if a man witnessed violence or was a target of violence as a child. Although this explanation has strengths, when we use it we tend to overlook the fact that women are usually available as role models of non-violent behavior. Yet boys, and adult men, do not commonly emulate women's behavior. A simple learning theory of battering will not suffice, because it does not explain why women are so often invisible to boys and men as models of how to be in relationships.

Battering is sometimes understood as a problem within the individual, such as the inability to recognize and express feelings. Another intra-personal explanation is that a man batters because he is unable to assertively express his needs and desires. It is true that some men who batter are poor at identifying and communicating feelings. However, Bill is not simply attempting to express a feeling when he says "you can't leave because you've been cheating on me." To account for Bill's behavior as an interpersonal communication problem is not convincing. He clearly knows what he wants, and is communicating it by words and action. Battering is not an inability to express feelings or wants, but a method by which a man does so.

When a man hits or yells at a woman, that is a choice he makes. No person or circumstance can make a man attack his partner verbally or physically.

Battering is sometimes seen as an anger management problem: a man is unable to express anger constructively. But Bill manages his anger quite effectively, using it as a weapon with which to batter. He directs it against women—not against the legal system or against his employer, for example. He also uses the fact that he was angry to help him get away with using abuse to control Janet. For instance, after physically battering Janet, Bill uses anger as a justification for his actions and shows feelings of regret and remorse to avoid any consequences of battering. Men who batter express feelings, including anger, when and to whom they want.

Analyzing Common Explanations

The fact that men who batter are able to manage skills such as communication and the expression of feelings allows that men may use these skills as tactics to batter. They are a part of battering rather than an explanation of battering. When a man is selective about when, where and to whom he is abusive, the implication is that battering is neither a communication problem nor an anger management problem, but a choice.

When a man hits or yells at a woman, that is a choice he makes. No person or circumstance can make a man attack his partner verbally or physically. There are circumstances which may increase the likelihood that a man will batter, but no circumstances make it inevitable that a man will make abusive choices. This means that explanations of battering which are interpersonal, such as communication issues or provocation, are inaccurate.

Men's power to batter women is not only personal; it flows from institutions whose social function is to set cultural norms and hold violators accountable.

Men, rather than circumstances, are responsible for abusive choices. Thus, an accurate explanation of battering would account for the reasons men make the choice to batter rather than an outside force that causes them to batter. In short, men batter to gain power and control over another person. This explanation is profound in that it frames individual acts of violence within a pattern of behavior. The explanation of power and control has become, however, something of a cliché, and its larger implications are overlooked. One often overlooked implication is that battering is purposeful. Men choose behavior in a systematic way in order to gain power and control. There is a function to a man's battering. That is, men batter in the short term to get a woman to do what he wants or to stop her from doing something.

When a man yells at a woman, criticizing her, he knows what effect his behavior will have on her. In the short term, his yelling will cause fear and pain, and in the longer term he will destroy her personhood so that he can have power and control over her. Men who batter know and choose the effects of battering. This is disturbing because it leaves us with the question, why do men want power and control?

Sexism as the Problem

Sexism is the source of men's choice to use violent and abusive tactics to gain power and control over a woman. The word "source" here means a wellspring, not a cause. Just as single incidents of violence are better understood within a pattern of that person's abusive behavior, so individual batterers are better understood within a social context of sexism. Within the context of sexism, it is inevitable, rather than unthinkable, that a large number of men will choose to use violence and abuse. The connection between sexism and men's violence can be better understood through a definition.

Sexism is gender prejudice + power. Gender prejudice is the predisposition to experience women as inferior to men. It is the filter through which men experience women's behavior as flawed, out of place, even evil. With such perceptions, men believe it is necessary to control women, and are willing to use violent and abusive choices to do so. Men's power to batter women is not only personal; it flows from institutions whose social function is to set cultural norms and hold violators accountable. Let's return to Bill for some examples to illustrate.

Understanding sexist beliefs and practices as the source of battering allows the community to work to prevent violence with a new clarity and resolve.

The first example looks at prejudice. Bill identified as his reason or justification for isolating Janet like this: Janet's friends are a bad influence on her, and she should stay away from them. Bill struggled with the connection of his justification to sexism. He eventually realized that he believed women are easily tempted and not trustworthy—that they need men to keep their moral compass pointed in the right direction. This belief led to his expectation that Janet check out her friends with him.

The source of Bill's beliefs is sexist social norms. When asked the sources of his belief that women are easily tempted and not trustworthy, Bill quickly answered, "The story of Eve" and pop psychology's characterization of women as "emotionally based" (unlike men are who "rationally based.") There is, then, a cascading effect from sexist cultural norms and messages about women to personally held beliefs about women, to expectations men have for women they are partnered with, to abuse and justifications when women act freely. Sexist norms and beliefs do not force any man to make the choice to be abusive, but they do provide the source from which such choices flow.

Adding Power to Sexism

Now let us look at power, the second part of our definition. The power men have to batter is increased by the sexism of institutions. As institutions set cultural norms, they have considerable power to name and define what is true. When institutions promote sexist messages about women, the seeming validity and reasonableness of Bill's beliefs increases. As a result, he has more power in the relationship to enforce his expectations as rules.

Institutional support is often a source of power unavailable for women. If Janet asserted before a congregation that she should make decisions for the family about who they see, she would not be taken as seriously as Bill. Institutions which name reality can increase the power men have to batter.

In addition to setting cultural norms, institutions are also responsible for holding violators of those norms accountable. However, when institutions promote sexist beliefs, they collude with men's control of women. This becomes a second source for increasing men's power over women. If the church accepts Bill's justification for his abuse, it colludes with him by supporting his belief that he has the right to control Janet. Janet receives an implicit message that her behavior is the problem—that if she doesn't follow Bill's rules, she's liable to be punished. This is one way in which institutional collusion can increase the power men have to batter.

Our summary definition, sexism = gender prejudice + power, says that men are prejudiced to experience women as inferior to themselves, and become willing to batter women. Institutions increase men's power to batter by setting sexist social norms, colluding with men who batter and implicitly holding women accountable for violating sexist norms.

Men's Resistance to Seeing Sexism as the Source of Battering

An understanding of sexism as the source of battering has implications for Bill, for other men and for the community. For Bill, the understanding that sexism is the source of his choice to batter means that his work to change is counter-cultural. Within a culture of sexism, controlling tactics are the expression of social norms, including chivalrous or deferential treatment. Genuinely respectful treatment of women is counter-cultural (respectful meaning honestly expressing ourselves and taking women seriously). In order to be respectful and safe towards women, Bill must work to change his beliefs, and to be aware of institutions which express sexist norms about women. If he does not change his beliefs, he may stop his violence for a period of time, but he will be merely "white knuckling"—in other words, restraining his desire to control Janet rather than working to have a non-abusive relationship with her.

The situation is much the same for all men. Like Bill, we are often resistant to the idea that sexism is the source of male violence. To accept this means having to face our commonalties with men who do batter. Both slapping a woman and dismissing her ideas flow from the same source—sexism. Such similarities can be more easily discounted if other explanations of battering are accepted. Acknowledging sexism means recognizing that we as men each have illegitimate power in male-female relationships. It means men share the problem and the benefits of battering, and the responsibility for ending it.

Understanding sexist beliefs and practices as the source of battering allows the community to work to prevent violence with a new clarity and resolve. Because violence is a choice, the community cannot create circumstances in which men will refrain from abuse. The community can, however, diminish men's prejudice and power by ending sexism. By diminishing prejudice, fewer men may make the choice to abuse women, and more men may be willing to treat women with respect. Additionally, diminishing sexism would change the context in which men make abusive choices. Men would be less able to justify abuse to the woman and to the community. As a result, when a man chose to be abusive and violent, perhaps he would be unable to have systematic power and control over a woman. In summary, any significant reduction in violence against women will entail addressing sexism as the source of men's battering.

CHAPTER 3

Are Current Approaches to Reducing Violence Against Women Effective?

Chapter Preface

In 1994, seven-year-old Megan Kanka was raped and asphyxiated by her thirty-three-year-old neighbor, Jesse Timmendequas, in Hamilton, New Jersey. This well-publicized case brought national attention to the issue of sexual violence against children. The investigation revealed that Mr. Timmendequas was a convicted child molester, and that two other paroled sex offenders lived near the Kanka family. "If I had known that three sex perverts were living across the street from me," said Mrs. Kanka, "Megan would be alive today."

Policy makers who agree with Mrs. Kanka have fought local, state, and national battles to make a sex offender's information accessible to the public. These efforts comprise one strategy among many to reduce violence against women and children. Sex offender registration laws require a convicted rapist or child molester to provide local law enforcement with a current address, phone number, social security number, and employment information. Some states also require fingerprints, a photograph, and a DNA sample. Those in favor of mandatory registration believe that sex offenders are less likely to commit another sex crime if they know that police can readily connect them to any new offense. California enacted the first sex offender registration law in 1947. By 1996 Congress passed the first version of legislation that required all states to have some form of registry in place or risk losing federal anticrime funding.

After Megan's tragedy, and several other sensational child molestation and rape cases in the 1990s, citizens began to demand more direct access to information about sex offenders. In order to actively take part in preventing crimes, neighborhoods organized to pass notification laws requiring law enforcement officials to alert residents whenever a sex offender moved into the area. These laws were designed to empower people to take proactive measures to protect themselves and their children. Siding with the pro-notification movement, Attorney General Janet Reno declared in 1997 that "accurate registries and effective community notification programs are at the heart of our fight against sex offenders."

In spite of Reno's confident assessment, registration and notification laws were controversial when they were first enacted, and they remain so today. Critics of registration laws contend that they do little to prevent sex crimes and that their real purpose is to inflict more punishment and revenge on offenders who have paid their debt to society. Those against notification laws claim that they are an unconstitutional assault on the ex-offender's right to privacy. They worry that such laws may increase recidivism because an offender is in danger of losing his job, housing, and community support if his past is made public. Even worse, critics say, giving free access to an offender's contact information may invite vigilantism. For example, in 2006 a nineteen-year-old man used the information he gathered on an online sex offender registry in Maine to find and then shoot down two offenders. When police apprehended him, they found that he had researched thirty-four sex offenders on his laptop computer, part of his plan to rid the state of rapists and molesters. Incidents like these have caused some states to remove or amend their notification legislation.

Much like the debate surrounding registration and notification laws, controversy often swirls around other methods and policies designed to reduce sexual violence and abuse of women. The viewpoints in the following chapter examine arguments for and against a variety of legal and social solutions to the problem of violence against women.

Better Enforcement of Mandatory Arrest Laws Reduces Domestic Violence

Jacqueline Seibel

Jacqueline Seibel is the police reporter for the Milwaukee Journal Sentinel *newspaper in Wisconsin.*

Women who call police to report domestic abuse are less likely to get arrested along with the suspect under the biggest change to Wisconsin's domestic abuse laws since mandatory arrests went into effect in 1989.

Previously, some officers had just been giving an abuse suspect a municipal ticket. As a result, suspects could be quickly released, sometimes sending them right back into their homes, said Patti Seger, executive director of the Wisconsin Coalition Against Domestic Violence.

Not anymore. Since April [2006], when the law took effect, police must take one of the parties involved to jail.

The majority of domestic violence incidents are between a man and a woman, and the majority of the predominant aggressors up to 95% are men, Seger said.

Dual Arrests

Activists against domestic violence saw another trend besides the more lenient civil ordinance citations being issued to abuse suspects: those reporting abuse being arrested along with abuse suspects. There have been far too many so-called dual arrests, Seger said.

Previously, the mandatory arrest law simply stated that the primary aggressor should be the person taken to jail. Some law enforcement agencies interpreted that to mean to arrest the person who hit first, Seger said.

There was nothing in the old law that discouraged dual arrests, meaning the person reporting abuse also could end up in jail.

"The victim of a crime by a stranger will likely do something to fend off the attacker," Seger said. "Why wouldn't someone in a domestic abuse situation do the same if they know what's coming?"

Reducing Dual Arrests

Seger said the changes effective on April 1 [2006] were necessary to prevent an abuse victim from being "re-victimized" in the law enforcement system and to stop law enforcement from shutting the door on the primary weapon many victims have—calling police for help.

Victims of abuse are less likely to call police if they believe they, too, will be arrested, Seger said.

'We're going to get back to protecting the victim.'

"Every law enforcement agency in the state is going to have to review its policy on domestic violence and incorporate the new law into their procedures," Brookfield Assistant Chief Dean Collins said. "The law is very clear."

The change was initiated because some of the state's 72 counties were reading the 1989 mandatory arrest law differently.

The new mandatory arrest dictate could have the greatest impact on public safety in communities with small police departments, which may have only one police officer on duty at a time.

Because the mandatory arrest means a jail trip, that can temporarily leave the community virtually unprotected.

It could also pose a problem for less populated counties where taking prisoners to jail can involve a 30-minute drive.

A Guideline for Arrests

Realizing that in some cases both parties should be arrested, advocates against domestic violence have set a nationwide guideline of 5% of all domestic violence incidents that will result in dual arrests.

Waukesha County has an arrest rate of 73% and a 10.2% dual arrest rate. Washington County has an arrest rate of 82.6% and reported one of the state's highest dual arrest rates, 16.9%, according to the 2003 *Wisconsin Department of Justice Domestic Abuse Incident Report*, the latest statistics available.

Milwaukee County has an arrest rate of 54% and did not report its dual arrests. Ozaukee County reported an arrest rate of 61.6% and zero dual arrests.

Washington County District Attorney Todd Martens said the 5% dual arrest guideline is arbitrary.

"Reality is much more complicated than that," he said. But he said the changes to the law are good, and that he has already started educating law enforcement officers about those changes.

Martens said his department handles about 400 domestic violence cases a year, and in every case, the people involved are required to meet in his office the day after the incident.

Waukesha County Sheriff's Capt. Karen Ruff said the department's policy on domestic violence has already been rewritten and distributed to all members. She supports the change.

"Although the domestic violence law always had a mandatory arrest element, some of that may have fallen to the wayside," Ruff said.

"We're going to get back to protecting the victim," she added.

Mixed Reviews

The changes to the law have had mixed reviews from the law enforcement establishment, which recognizes it will mean more training and new procedures.

Waukesha police Capt. Mike Babe said the new law will likely mean more overtime and more time spent on domestic violence calls.

"It's jail or bail," Babe said.

Waukesha police respond to about 300 domestic disputes a year. Officers always separate the parties and bring at least one of them to the police station.

In the past, sometimes separating the parties was deemed to be enough intervention. It had been a judgment call by officers, he said.

Brookfield Assistant Chief Collins said domestic abuse situations involve a decision-making balance by officers because arresting two people ties up officers for a longer time than arresting one. Also, officers will be spending more time during the initial investigation to determine who was the predominant aggressor, he noted.

Determining the predominant aggressor could be even trickier in the case of roommates or same-gender disputes, officials said.

Questions for Police to Consider:

1. Is there a history of abuse?
2. What do witnesses say occurred?
3. Are there injuries?
4. Does one party seem to fear the other?
5. Is one person making threats?
6. Did one party act in self-defense?

The Violence Against Women Act Is Necessary to Protect Women

Jill J. Morris on Behalf of The National Coalition Against Domestic Violence

The National Coalition Against Domestic Violence brings together the collective power of leaders, individuals, and communities to innovate methods and programs to end domestic violence.

The Violence Against Women Act (VAWA) is a revolutionary piece of legislation that has greatly improved the criminal justice and community-based responses to domestic violence, dating violence, sexual assault and stalking in the United States. The passage of VAWA in 1994 and its reauthorization in 2000 has dramatically changed the landscape for victims who once suffered in silence. Because of VAWA's programs, victims have been able to access services, and a new generation of families and justice system professionals have come to understand that domestic violence, dating violence, sexual assault and stalking are crimes that our society will not tolerate. . . .

How VAWA Provides Legal Services for Victims

Funding for civil legal assistance has allowed the legal professionals of Center for Community Solutions [CCS] provide confidential assistance to victims of domestic violence, sexual assault, and stalking for the last five years. Since 2001, when CCS received its first funding through the Legal Assistance for Victims [LAV] grant from the Office on Vio-

Jill J. Morris, *Written Testimony on the Violence Against Women Act of 2005, on Behalf of The National Coalition Against Domestic Violence, as Presented to U.S. Senate Committee on the Judiciary*, July 19, 2005. http://www.ncadv.org/files/NCADVSenate TestimonyS1197.pdf. Reproduced by permission.

lence Against Women, attorneys and advocates of the Legal Department have assisted thousands of victims, allowing them to escape from abusive and violent relationships, achieve safety by breaking the cycle of violence, and access legal and social justice for themselves and their children. The essential live-changing and life-saving services that LAV funding has allowed CCS to provide includes assistance with restraining orders and safety planning, family law matters (divorce, paternity, child custody/support, etc.), court accompaniment (for emotional support), California Safe at Home confidential address program applications, consultations and referrals for battered immigrant spouse petitions and U.S. visa applications, as well as general legal consultations/referrals. The importance of civil legal assistance for victims of domestic violence cannot be overstated. Explaining the recent decline in national domestic violence incidents, the April 2003 issue of the *Journal of Contemporary Economic Policy* stated that "the increased provision of legal services for victims of intimate partner abuse" was the single most important factor. In sum, VAWA has saved lives and improved the lives of thousands.

> *Steve Allen, Counselor at Law Center for Community,*
> *Solutions San Diego, California*

In September 2005, the Violence Against Women Act will expire.[1] Without this critical legislation our communities will lose billions of dollars in Federal resources that not only save lives but promote overall safety and security of our homes and citizens.

Statistics show:

- One in every 4 women will experience domestic violence during her lifetime.

- Women are almost 6 times as likely as men to be victims of rape or attempted rape in their lifetime. While 9 out of 10 rape victims are women, men and boys are also victims of sexual assault.

1. Editor's Note: The VAWA was reauthorized by Congress in October 2005.

- 40 to 60% of men who abuse women also abuse children.

- 64% of women who report being raped, physically assaulted, and/or stalked since age 18 were victimized by a current or former intimate partner.

- Women ages 16 to 24 experience the highest per capita rates of intimate violence.

- In 1994, approximately 37% of women seeking injury-related treatment in hospital emergency rooms were there because of injuries inflicted by a current or former spouse or intimate partner.

- One survey found that over 50% of abused women lost at least three days of work each month due to abuse.

This year [2005], Congress has a unique opportunity not only to continue successful and crucial existing VAWA programs, but also to expand on ten years of progress to further the safety and stability of the lives of survivors of domestic violence, dating violence, sexual assault and stalking.

VAWA's Ten Years of Success

The Violence Against Women Act has created innovative, multi-disciplinary, coordinated community responses to domestic violence and sexual assault, which address the many needs and fill in the vast gaps identified by the experts. VAWA has supported police, judges, advocates and victim service providers, VAWA created new federal criminal laws addressing domestic violence and established discretionary grant programs within the Department of Justice and the Department of Health and Human Services for state, local, and Tribal governments and non-profit service organizations. VAWA of 2000 renewed these programs, made targeted improvements to certain provisions and introduced new initiatives. Over the past decade these programs and new laws have proven essential to intervening and preventing intimate partner violence in our communities. . . .

How VAWA Can Continue to Help Victims of Sexual Assault

As a Board member for our new, local sexual assault services program, VAWA has most definitely filled a void. Until recently, our rural area had *no* services for rape victims, and VAWA funding has been a major part in bringing such services to fruition.

Pat Peterson Peace Place, Winder, Georgia

In 1994 and 2000, VAWA reauthorized the Health and Human Services Rape Prevention and Education Program. A part of Preventative Health Services Block Grant funding, this specialized program helps states address sexual assault by funding education and prevention initiatives such as seminars and rape crisis hotlines. This is a formula program available to each state with amounts dependent on population. At least 25% of the funds must be targeted to middle school, junior high and high school students. This program is essential to the reauthorization of VAWA in 2005.

Approximately 1,315 rape crisis centers across the country help victims of rape, sexual assault, sexual abuse, and incest rebuild their lives by providing a range of vital services to victims. These centers:

• Operate 24-hour hotlines

• Provide 24-hour accompaniment to law enforcement departments, hospitals, and legal proceedings

• Offer short- and long-term individual counseling and support groups for victims and their families

• Assist victims with obtaining compensation and restitution

Rape crisis centers serve all victims of sexual violence, including women who have been raped, child sexual assault and incest survivors, adult survivors of childhood sexual abuse, male victims, persons with disabilities, and victims who experience abuse in later life. They also provide necessary aid to family members and others affected by sexual violence.

The effectiveness of such supportive interventions has been documented. Studies have found that services such as those provided by our nation's rape crisis centers can shorten the amount of time a person exhibits symptoms of rape-related posttraumatic stress disorder. In addition, victims who receive information and services are more likely to participate in the criminal justice process.

Domestic Violence and the Workplace

Economic security is one of the most formidable obstacles for survivors of domestic violence, sexual violence and stalking. Not only does domestic violence have economic effects on individuals, communities and families, but economic dependence can prohibit victims from seeking safety or services. Many abusers attempt to retain power over their victims through economic control, and will often attempt to sabotage a victim's ability to work productively.

Abused or trafficked non-citizens often face multiple barriers when trying to escape a violent relationship.

Recent studies have found that between 35 and 56 percent of employed battered women surveyed were harassed at work by their abusers. A 1998 study by the Government Accountability Office found that between one quarter and one half of domestic violence victims report having lost a job due in part to domestic violence. Likewise, almost half of sexual assault survivors lost their jobs or were forced to quit in the aftermath of the crime, and more than 35 percent of stalking victims report losing time from work due to the stalking and seven percent never return to work.

By authorizing Title VII of VAWA 2005, the Senate will help victims maintain their role in the workplace and assist businesses in achieving greater productivity. For example, by providing emergency unpaid leave to victims of domestic violence and sexual assault, Congress can ensure that victims are able to obtain the legal, medical, and social services necessary for them to escape violence. Having a steady source of income can make all the difference in whether a survivor establishes economic independence or returns to their abuser.

Victims report that they have been fired from their jobs for taking time off to obtain an order of protection, attend court proceedings, or find emergency housing. Title VII, which entitles victims to ten days of emergency unpaid leave to attend to these needs, will ensure that survivors of domestic violence are not forced to choose between retaining employment and escaping violence.

Furthermore, employers will benefit from VAWA 2005 by providing emergency unpaid leave to victims of domestic and sexual violence, employers will face fewer turnovers in the workplace. Currently, victims of intimate partner violence lose 8,000,000 days of paid work each year—the equivalent of over 32,000 full-time jobs and 5,600,000 days of household productivity. Unpaid emergency leave would make it more likely that employees could stay at work while they dealt with the violence, or return to work more quickly following the emergency leave. Overall, these provisions would facilitate a net rise in productivity, and businesses would benefit from the increasing rates of return from a safer and more stable workforce. . . .

Protecting Battered Immigrant Women

In 1994 and 2000, VAWA set out to remove obstacles inadvertently interposed by immigration law that would prevent non-citizen victims from safely escaping domestic violence. Over the past ten years, the immigration provisions in VAWA have helped victims fleeing abusive relationships and have limited the ability of abusers, traffickers, and perpetrators of sexual assault to paralyze their victims with threats of deportation. VAWA 2005 builds upon the already solid foundation established over the past decade and provides expanded improvements and technical corrections to further ensure the safety of non-citizen and trafficked victims of domestic violence.

Research has found that between 34 and 49.5% of immigrant women experience domestic violence over the course of their lifetimes. Immigrant married women experience higher levels of domestic violence (59.5%) and research has found that over 50% of immigrant women surveyed were still living with their abusers. Abused or trafficked non-citizens often face multiple barriers when trying to escape a violent relationship. When attempting to leave some victims face obstacles and complications, such as: a combination of language barriers, cultural differences, citizenship status, and lack of access to services. These barriers all attribute to the fear and frustration that victims face when attempting to leave an abuser. Because of these complex barriers, non-citizens and trafficked persons are particularly vulnerable to becoming victims of domestic violence.

Native women are more likely to be battered, raped, and stalked than any other group of women.

In 1994, VAWA recognized the special circumstances and hardships that can apply to non-citizen survivors of domestic abuse, and it provided avenues to allow abused spouses and children to leave their abusive families without jeopardizing their immigration status. VAWA 2000 expanded upon those provisions and provided additional relief for non-citizen survivors including new types of visas for survivors of trafficking, sexual assault, and other crimes. The immigration provisions in VAWA 2005 are designed to build upon the successes of VAWA provisions in 1994 and 2000. These provisions provide new forms of immigration relief to domestic abuse and/or trafficking survivors and addressing specialized needs are certain categories of immigrants such as the Nicaraguan Adjustment and Central American Relief Act (NACARA).

VAWA 2005 includes several vital provisions necessary for the protection of battered non-citizens and trafficked victims. VAWA 2005 seeks to prevent the Department of Homeland Security from seizing victims of domestic violence, sexual assault, and trafficking while they seek services at battered women shelters, rape crisis centers and protection order courts. One of the main reasons battered non-citizens refuse to seek assistance is out of fear they will automatically be turned over to immigration authorities. By preventing immigration officials from removing victims from these safe havens, victims will be more likely to seek out such service and receive assistance. . . .

Domestic Violence and Communities of Color

Domestic violence, dating violence, sexual assault, and stalking impact people of all ages, cultures, and socio-economic status. Although the Violence Against Women Act has provided increased protection and resources for victims, racial and ethnic minorities often have limited access to these crucial services. VAWA 2005 must support communities of color in their development of culturally and linguistically appropriate services that meet the needs of the community.

Many women of color encounter barriers to accessing appropriate services for domestic violence, dating violence, sexual assault, and stalking. Language barriers and cultural differences prevent many women of color from accessing services that offer protection for them and their children. Frequently, the nearest victim service provider is outside their community and may not embrace the woman's culture or adequately address the woman's safety needs of their communities. Community organizations and domestic violence, dating violence, sexual assault, and stalking organizations must develop culturally-specific services, offered in the victim's native language.

Provisions for culturally-specific services developed within communities of color are included in all titles of VAWA 2005. The definition of underserved communities includes racial and ethnic populations. The bill ensures adequate distribution of funds to programs serving communities of color. VAWA 2005 fosters collaboration between culturally-specific community organizations and domestic violence, dating violence, sexual assault and stalking organizations. In addition, VAWA 2005 requires grantees to collaborate with representatives from racial, ethnic and other underserved communities to develop and implement new programs. Grant applicants must document their programs' impact on racial, ethnic, and other underserved communities and include this information in plans and reports. Also, this bill allocates a coalition set-aside as well as other funds to organizations within United States Territories that address domestic violence, dating violence, sexual assault, and stalking. . . .

Domestic Violence and Native Americans

Native women are more likely to be battered, raped, and stalked than any other group of women. Native women are three times more likely to be physically assaulted than Caucasian women. Native women experience sexual assault at more than twice the rate of Caucasian women, three times the rate of Hispanic women, and seven times the rate of Asian women. Authorizing the Tribal programs in VAWA 2005 is of particular importance given the heightened rate of violence against American Indian and Alaska Native women.

To gain a better understanding of these devastating rates of violence, Title IX, authorizes the National Institute of Justice to conduct a study focused on domestic violence, dating violence, sexual assault, stalking, and murder in Indian country. This comprehensive study will both identify obstacles and make recommendations on how to better prevention efforts, community response and prosecution of these crimes. Upon the study's completion, a task force of tribal leaders and victim's rights advocates will assemble to determine how to best implement the study's recommendations. This research and analysis will provide new direction to the movement to end violence against Native women.

VAWA 2005 will also establish a Deputy Director for Tribal Affairs in the Office on Violence Against Women. The Deputy Director will ensure that a portion of tribal set-aside funds are used to develop and maintain tribal domestic violence shelters or programs for battered Indian women; create new tribal education awareness programs and materials that address violence against Indian women; and to enhance the response of Indian tribes to respond to crimes including legal services for victims and Indian-specific offender programs.

Changing Male Attitudes Reduces Sexual Violence

Christopher Kilmartin

*Christopher Kilmartin is a professor of psychology at Mary Wash-
ington College in Fredericksburg, Virginia, and a nationally recognized expert on the psychology of men.*

April [2006] is Sexual Assault Awareness Month, and too
often we see domestic violence and rape defined as
"women's issues." Since men do the vast majority of the damage, I think it's a men's issue. I'll begin with a story, not a very
happy one, to set the tone.

A little while back, the *Washington Post* ran a story about a
Northern VA country club that held an event called the "Vodka
challenge." It was a men-only event, a standard country club
golf tournament. What made it newsworthy was the mode of
celebration in the men's locker room. The day before the tournament, one of the club managers purchased an ice sculpture
of a nude woman, sitting down with her legs spread. The
vodka was served in the locker room from a fountain stream
that came out from between her legs.

When some of the women members found out about this
ice sculpture, they were outraged. Most of the men seemed
puzzled by this reaction. After all, this was a sculpture, not a
real woman, and it was in the men's locker room, where none
of the women would even see it. Quite predictably, there were
a lot of statements about angry feminists who have no sense
of humor, and the overly rigid atmosphere of political correctness. After all, any one with an open mind would see this
as harmless. I think it's good to have an open mind, but it's
not good to have a mind so open that your brain falls out.

Christopher Kilmartin, "Editorial: Men's Violence Against Women," *The Society for the
Psychological Study of Men and Masculinity (SPSMM) Bulletin*, vol. 10, Spring 2006.
http://www.apa.org/divisions/div51/div51/01.htm. Reproduced by permission of the author.

What does this vodka challenge story have to do with violence against women? There was nothing in the story to suggest that any of these men had ever beaten their wives. But, although I'm sure they didn't realize it, every one of them made it just a little more possible for any one of them to commit an act of violence against a woman.

The two most frequent crimes against women are largely invisible to the media.

In order for violence to occur, several things have to be present. First, there has to be a lack of identification with the victim. Second, there has to be a perception of the situation as one that calls for violence. Third, there has to be a decision to act violently, and fourth, there has to be a means of doing harm to the other person.

Devaluing Women

All-male social groups that are disrespectful towards women provide the first part of this formula: a willingness to view women as being different from and less valued than men. Symbolically, the ice sculpture provided an atmosphere that says women are here for men's pleasure, and we will bond around our shared masculinity in this place where we don't have to deal with women as human beings. Seeing them as lower status others allows us to justify mistreating them in many ways, including violence. There is an attitudinal undercurrent of women as enemies, in spite of the fact that most of these men were married to and raising children with the enemy.

Unfortunately, this vodka challenge was most likely not some isolated incident of insensitivity. In fact, country clubs have a history of the exclusion and disrespect of women, from men-only eating areas and tee times to the outright banning of women members. Many clubs also have a history of excluding Jews and people of color. The controversy over the exclusion of women from Augusta National is a case in point—[feminist and political psychologist] Martha Burk has been called every bad name in the book just because she has pointed out the bigotry of this incredibly wealthy group of men and suggested that we all do something to ensure that they don't become wealthier from the Master's tournament.

Condoning Violence, Fueling Fear

I am only using country clubs as an example of all-male enclaves that implicitly and subtly condone violence against women. Other institutions, like many fraternities and corporations, also have these histories. And, of course, all-male social groups do not have to be organized and institutional to provide this violence-condoning atmosphere. We can find informal men's groups in workplaces, college dorms, athletic teams, and corner bars, telling demeaning jokes about women, calling them by animal names or the names of their genitals, and these men rarely confront each other for fear of being attacked or ostracized. There is an unconscious, implicit conspiracy in many men's groups to keep women in their place. What better way to do it than by causing them to feel perpetually fearful of being physically attacked?

Men's violence is the single most serious health problem for women in the United States. It causes more harm than accidents, muggings, and cancer combined. For women aged 15–44, an estimated 50% of emergency room visits are the result of violence at the hands of their husbands, boyfriends, ex-husbands, or ex-boyfriends. Every year male partners or ex-partners murder more than 1000 women—that's about 3 per day. It happens so often that people don't even pay attention to it. When a stranger murders someone, the story is on the front page of the metro section. If it's an intimate, it's at the bottom of page 4. A stranger rape always makes the papers; an acquaintance rape never does unless the rapist is somebody famous. The two most frequent crimes against women are largely invisible to the media. We expect it so much that we don't even notice it.

Men's violence is considered to be a given, and women's responses to that violence are seen as choices. This subtly makes women responsible for the violence.

I want to point out that I chose my words very carefully there. I very intentionally did not say "when a person is murdered by a stranger." Maybe it's just because I'm a college professor, but I am an absolute believer in the power of language, and there is some everyday language that smuggles in prejudices against women and contributes to the cultural atmosphere that enables gender-based violence. I have 5 examples.

The Power of Language to Perpetuate Violence

The first is the one I just pointed out—passive voice—1000 women are murdered. The victim, not the perpetrator, is the subject of the sentence. When you see this language often enough, the perpetrator becomes a kind of afterthought. Imagine if sportscasters talked like this: "The score was tied when a three-point basket was scored." "Many dollars were earned." Wouldn't everyone ask, "Who did it? Who is responsible?"

Example #2: the use of the term "opposite sex" and the phrase "battle of the sexes". I challenge you to tell me one way in which the sexes are opposite. Calling men and women opposites is like calling an IBM computer the opposite of an Apple. And "battle of the sexes" implies that men and women are at war. We will never solve this problem until we work together and emphasize our commonalities rather than our differences.

I see research studies reported in the popular press—"a recent study proves what we have suspected all along—that men's and women's brains are different." And what they do is find some infinitesimally small portion of the brain that has some minor difference that accounts for 5% of the variance in a population with wide variability, completely ignoring the fact that men's and women's brains both have frontal cortex, amygdalas, thalamuses, hypothalamuses, and on and on. And at the end of the story, the anchorman on the news says, "Well, that explains why I can't understand my wife at all." (If you can t understand your wife, I recommend the much-overlooked method of listening to her).

Example #3, when I tell people I'm a psychologist specializing in gender-based violence, people always ask, when a man is beating his wife, why does she stay with him? That's question #2; they never ask question #1: Why would a man hit his wife? Men's violence is considered to be a given, and women's responses to that violence are seen as choices. This subtly makes women responsible for the violence.

It is vitally important that we, as men of conscience, take seriously our role in ending sexual violence.

Example #4: self-defense classes for women that are advertised as "rape prevention." Is it women's job to prevent rape? Don't get me wrong—I'm all for women learning self-defense if they want to, but let's call it what it really is—risk reduction. It is men's responsibility to prevent rape.

Example #5 comes from the recent scandal over sexual assaults at the Air Force Academy. It turns out that there were numerous male cadets who have sexually assaulted female cadets, and the men who run the Academy intimidated survivors into keeping silent about it. The newspaper stories said something like, 54 rapes occurred between male and female cadets. I'm sorry—rapes do not occur between people. Does a bank robbery occur between a robber and a teller? Does vandalism occur between a kid with a can of spray paint and somebody's property? And here's another flash of brilliance—in reaction to the scandal, the head of the academy said that the problem was that men and women live in the same residence hall and that men would see women walking down the hall in their bathrobes, and that he was going to now have the men and women living in separate residence halls. So, let's get this straight: the problem is that men are raping women and so the solution is to get rid of the women?! It's a new height in victim-blaming. I know I get out of control when I see a woman in a bathrobe. How does that work, physiologically? Prostate exerts pressure on the spinal cord, cutting off oxygen to the brain? And, newspapers reported the Air Force problem as a "sex scandal." I would submit that the victims were not having sex, and we could also argue that the perpetrators were not either.

Men Should Confront Sexism

When we see gender-based violence, women-hating is just around the corner. Therefore, if we can turn this attitude around, we can go a long way toward solving this problem. And, the people who are in the best position to do so are men—we have the social status, power, and privilege. We can speak out and affect the attitudes of our fellow men. Just as white people have a special role to play in ending racism, rich people have a special role to play in ending economic inequality, and heterosexuals have a special role to play in ending homophobia, it is vitally important that we, as men of conscience, take seriously our role in ending sexual violence.

In the locker room at the vodka challenge that day, I'm betting that there was at least one man who was uncomfortable with this ice sculpture, just as there is when someone hires a stripper for a bachelor party or makes a woman the butt of a joke. It's not unlikely that more than one man felt this way. But nobody spoke up because each man feels that he may be the only one, and taking on the collective opinion of the rest of the group can leave him out in the cold. There is tremendous pressure to laugh along with the boys or at least not say anything. It would have taken tremendous courage for a man to stand up and say, even matter-of-factly, "That ice sculpture is really offensive; what could you have been thinking? Why don't we just get rid of it before we're all embarassed? We can have just as much fun without it." And it's ironic to me that courage is supposed to be a hallmark of masculinity, but there are so many men who find it impossible to display this kind of courage. They would sooner run into a burning building or have a fist fight. Men are also supposed to be independent, but there is tremendous conformity in most all-male peer groups, whether they are adults or younger men.

'Boys will be boys' not only provides a measure of excuse for violence against women, it is a very disrespectable attitude toward men.

Social psychologists have known for a long time that one of the biggest barriers to being able to disagree with a group is unanimity. When the group opinion is unanimous and you don't have an ally, the pressure to conform is tremendous. But if even one person voices a disagreement with the rest of the group, others are much more likely to follow suit. There were probably several uncomfortable men in that locker room that day. If one of them had spoken out, he might have found that there was more support in the room than he had imagined. But somebody has got to go first. Somebody has got to take a risk. Someone has to be the leader. It's masculine to take a risk, to be a leader; why are so few of us doing it? The research indicates that 75% of college men are uncomfortable when their male peers display these kinds of attitudes. Most men don't like it; we need to let other men know that we don't.

Changing Assumptions About Men

Along with changing our attitudes toward women, we've also got to change our attitudes toward ourselves. For several years, I have been involved in efforts to fight the alarming prevalence of sexual assault on college campuses. When this problem was first identified in the 1970s, colleges began to provide self-defense training, teach women how to avoid dangerous situations, and provide better lighting and emergency phones across the campus. Obviously, these are very important measures. But, these kinds of strategies constituted the basic extent of campus programming for about twenty years, and all of these measures have one thing in common: they only address potential victims. It is only been the last few years that people have begun to try to do something about the potential perpetrators? Why did it take us so long to come to this obviously important strategy? I think it is the pervasive perception boys will be boys and the only thing we can do is to wait until they commit a crime, and then put them in jail. Some still consider rape an act of male sexuality gone awry, rather than an act of violence. But we know different, just as we know that if a person hits another person over the head with a frying pan, we don't call that cooking.

If men's violent behavior is perceived as an unchangeable constant, then violence toward women is a women's issue, never a men's issue. "Boys will be boys" not only provides a measure of excuse for violence against women, it is a very disrespectable attitude toward men, as if we are animals, with absolutely no control over ourselves. And again, there's an irony here. Self-control is another hallmark of traditional masculinity, but aggression and sexuality are considered to be completely out of control—a man's gotta do what a man's gotta do. I want men to have more dignity than that. I saw this book title recently, "All men are jerks until proven otherwise." It made me sad—and I also realized, how am I ever going to prove what I'm not? Maybe I was a nice guy today, but who knows what's going to happen tomorrow. It's a sad state of affairs when so many men have behaved so irresponsibly that the rest of us have to carry the burden of understandable suspicion from women.

So, besides becoming more respectful toward women, we have to regain our self-respect. We are human beings who are capable of caring for others. We are not animals who lash out instinctively, poisoned by testosterone. Violence against women is a men's issue, and men have to take a leadership role in building a more positive male community. A man's gotta do what a man's gotta do.

Mandatory Arrest Laws Do Not Reduce Domestic Violence

Richard L. Davis

Richard L. Davis is a criminology instructor at Quincy College in Plymouth, Massachusetts. He is the author of Domestic Violence: Facts and Fallacies *and numerous articles for newspapers, journals, and magazines about domestic violence.*

There is nothing as deceptive as an obvious fact.

—Sir Arthur Conan Doyle

The indifference of law enforcement is the reason given for mandatory arrest policies. That is a false premise. Allegations and data that suggest officers refuse to arrest perpetrators ignore the facts. Often statute law denied officers the right of arrest and often offenders are absent when officers arrive. In the vast majority of minor assaults, in general or domestic violence cases in particular, officers would listen to the desires of those who had been assaulted.

Because of contemporary mandatory arrest, minor "family conflict" must be treated the same as violent "battering behavior." In approximately half the states, arrest is mandated regardless of how minor the assault, ignoring the desire of families and despite the fact that the incident is an isolated act of minor family conflict.

Battering Versus Family Conflict

Most researchers agree that a "batterer" is a family member or intimate partner who with premeditation and malice aforethought repeatedly uses coercion, force or violent physical assaults to manipulate and control the behavior of another

Richard L. Davis, "Mandatory Arrest: A Law Enforcement Nightmare," *Men's News Daily*, July 13, 2005. http://www.mensnewsdaily.com/archive/ce/davis/2005/davis 071305.htm. Reproduced by permission.

family member or intimate partner. Research documents that "batterers" are dangerous people and they deserve to be arrested.

Studies document that many families have discovered that mandatory arrest that ignores the context of the incident, can have unintended detrimental effects on families.

Family conflict most often occurs without premeditation or malice aforethought and involves the use of threats and/or minor physical assault in a specific or isolated disagreement. This behavior is often the result of perceived misbehavior, financial matters, jealously, anger or personality disorders.

The *National Violence Against Women Survey* documents that more than half of all physical assaults by intimates are relatively minor and consist of pushing, grabbing, shoving, slapping and hitting and that 1.3% of women and 0.9% of men are physically assaulted by an intimate partner annually.

A June 2005 Department of Justice (DOJ) report, *Family Violence Statistics*, documents that family violence accounts for only 11% of all reported and unreported violence and the majority of family violence is simple assault. Less than one half of one percent of family violence is fatal.

Some of the millions of family members who engage in minor family conflict may require law enforcement intervention. However, studies document that many families have discovered that mandatory arrest that ignores the context of the incident, can have unintended detrimental effects on families.

Ideology Trumps Science

On July 3, 2005 Senator Joe Biden on [the TV show] *Face the Nation* said, "The last thing we need in this country is ideological purity." Biden ignores the fact that the only foundation for mandatory arrest is gender feminist "ideological purity."

Mandatory arrest has little to no support from criminologists nor do empirical studies document its efficacy.

Men battering women is what most people think of when they hear the term "domestic violence." However, data document "family conflict" occurs far more often than "battering." Michael P. Johnson, a respected feminist researcher, believes that it is scientifically and ethically immoral not to distinguish between minor and serious abusive behavior.

Requiring arrest for everyone may reduce the resources of communities when they respond to chronic violent offenders and victims most at risk.

Studies document that the majority of scholars and researchers agree with Johnson. It is apparent that our public policy makers and many domestic violence advocates are either ignorant of these studies or have, for ideological reasons, decided to disagree.

The Drawbacks of Mandatory Arrest

Mandatory arrest demands that officers ignore the diverse needs and desires of families and it removes the option of choice. That power is placed into the absentee hands of "a state that claims it knows best." Arrest is paramount, logic and reason are secondary.

The National Research Council study, *Advancing the Federal Research Agenda on Violence Against Women*, notes that there are dangers in not distinguishing between an act of violence, abuse or battering.

The DOJ sponsored study, *Police Intervention and the Repeat of Domestic Assault*, document that sometimes police intervention is necessary, however, the effect of arrest is too small to have policy significance.

The DOJ report *Forgoing Criminal Justice Assistance: The Non-Reporting of New Incidents of Abuse in a Court Sample of*

Domestic Violence Victims documents that for some families, mandatory arrest and one-size-fits-all criminal justice-policies can be more harmful than helpful.

The DOJ study, *The Effects of Arrest on Intimate Partner Violence: New Evidence From the Spouse Assault Replication Program* documents that officers and families should have the choice concerning arrest because the majority of offenders discontinue their aggressive behavior without an arrest.

It concludes that requiring arrest for everyone may reduce the resources of communities when they respond to chronic violent offenders and victims most at risk. The authors also believe that research needs to assess the benefits and costs of mandatory arrest before implementing mandatory arrest policies.

Some mandatory arrests can become a nightmare for families and law enforcement agencies. DOJ studies document that it is time that our public policy makers re-think this one-size-fits-all, ideologically based intervention.

The Violence Against Women Act Is Unconstitutional

Stephen Baskerville

Stephen Baskerville is president of the nonprofit American Coalition of Fathers and Children and the author of Taken into Custody: The War Against Fathers, Marriage, and the Family *and numerous articles about men's rights for popular and scholarly publications.*

Tyrants and totalitarians never lack excuses for new forms of tyranny, and they are usually good ones: "necessity," "public safety," "the poor"—these have been standard throughout history. With the rise of feminism, the rationale has become, "It's for the children"—or sometimes, "women and children."

The Violence Against Women Act (VAWA), currently up for renewal, is possibly the most totalitarian measure ever passed by the Congress. Every jurisdiction has criminal statutes punishing violent assault. So why do we need a law punishing assaults specifically "against women"? Why must it be a federal law, for which no constitutional authority exists? And why is $4 billion in taxpayers' money required to outlaw something that is already against the law? The answer, as usual, is power—power for those who promise to protect us against yet another new danger.

It is politically hazardous for politicians to question any measure marketed for women and children. But no evidence indicates any problem of violence specifically against women. A virtually unanimous body of research has demonstrated that domestic violence is perpetrated by both sexes in roughly equal measures. So what is the real agenda behind this bill?

Feminist Propaganda

First, it politicizes criminal justice and redefines crime according to feminist ideology. Similar to "hate crimes" laws, criminals are designated not by their deeds but by their gender. As the act's title makes clear, only women qualify as victims. Violence against men is permissible. Both genders are equal, but one is more equal than the other.

VAWA destroys families and leaves children fatherless by providing weapons for divorce and custody battles.

Supporters like Senator Joseph Biden hem and haw that, despite the name, VAWA applies to both sexes. Yet they adamantly oppose explicitly gender-inclusive language. This is self-refuting, like the joke about the bad restaurant where the food is inedible and the portions are too small.

The "crimes" too are defined not by their statutory illegality but by ideology. VAWA allows men to be arrested and prosecuted for "violence" that is not violent: "name-calling and constant criticizing, insulting, and belittling the victim," "blaming the victim for everything," "ignoring, dismissing, or ridiculing the victim's needs."

Funding Feminist Advocacy and Destroying the Family

VAWA also funds political advocacy. It creates programs to "educate" (the old Maoist euphemism for indoctrinate) police, prosecutors, judges, and other officials in feminist ideology, so they will administer not equal justice but feminist justice.

VAWA circumvents the Bill of Rights. Criminal assault charges require due process of law, but labeling something "domestic violence" allows officials to ignore constitutional protections: the presumption of innocence is cast aside; hearsay evidence is admissible; no jury trial is required; the accused cannot face their accusers; even forced confessions are permissible. These are the methods being used in the burgeoning system of feminist "domestic violence courts" that are created for no reason other than to bypass civil liberties protections and railroad men into jail.

Further, VAWA mandates "restraining orders" that do not punish criminals for illegal acts but prohibit law-abiding citizens from otherwise legal ones. Judges can simply legislate new crimes on the spot. But they are only crimes for some people, who can then be arrested for doing what no law prohibits and what others may do.

Finally, VAWA destroys families and leaves children fatherless by providing weapons for divorce and custody battles. It is common knowledge among legal practitioners that trumped-up accusations are rampant and even encouraged in divorce courts. "The number of women attending seminars [on divorce by bar associations] who smugly—indeed boastfully—announced that they had already sworn out false or grossly exaggerated domestic violence complaints against their hapless husbands, and that the device worked!" astonished author Thomas Kiernan, writing in the *New Jersey Law Journal.* "To add amazement to my astonishment, the lawyer-lecturers invariably congratulated the self-confessed miscreants." The feminists' own literature reveals the true agenda. A special issue of *Mother Jones* magazine ostensibly on domestic violence is devoted, from the first paragraph, largely to securing child custody.

Growing Opposition

A chorus of opposition to VAWA has arisen. Heads of major pro-family organizations have written Congress warning of the dangers and urging changes. Yet the juggernaut rolls on, promoted from the inside by judges and civil servants who are supposed to be apolitical but whose lobbying is financed by VAWA itself.

VAWA represents the dangerous acceptance of extremist ideology by the mainstream. As recently as 1999, *Mother Jones* published a reasonably balanced report on the gender breakdown of domestic violence. By contrast, the recent issue is a screed, a vicious hate campaign by an extremist sect that abandons all pretence of objectivity and accuracy—and which, astoundingly, is being implemented by the US Congress.

Domestic Violence Treatment Is Gender Biased

Wendy McElroy

Wendy McElroy defines herself as an individual feminist and is the author of numerous books and articles, including XXX: A Woman's Right to Pornography *and* Sexual Correctness: The Gender Feminist Attack on Women.

The oldest battered women's shelter in New England, established in 1975, is setting precedent and making many feminists nervous in the process.

Transition House not only launched a "gender-neutral" search for a new executive director but also appointed a man as its interim director. Transition House explains that it simply wants to hire the best person for the job, and interviewing men doubles the chance of success.

Feminists of my ilk, who judge individuals on merit rather than gender, are applauding. (Admittedly, a muttered "it's about time!" may also be heard.)

Feminists who believe that gender must be a deciding factor in who addresses domestic violence and how it should be addressed, are appalled. They view the very prospect of hiring a male director as violating the "mission" of the shelter movement: to assist battered women and children.

In short, the "women-only feminists" believe males should be precluded from major employment and entry at shelters. Indeed, women's shelters often deny entry to male children over 12 years old. (The legality of doing so at tax-funded shelters is dubious, to say the least.)

Justifications for the Exclusion of Men

Why should even male teenagers be excluded? In a protest letter to the Transition House Board, the feminist organization

Wendy McElroy, "Gender Bias in Domestic Violence Treatment," *ifeminists.com* August 31, 2005. Reproduced by permission.

About Women explained that the shelter must be a space where "women could feel safe from male intrusion and could openly unburden themselves of the experiences of male violence they had undergone without fear of censure, criticism or inhibition by male presence."

Women-only feminists argue that women are battered not merely by an individual male abuser but by the entire male gender.

One interpretation of the foregoing statement makes sense. Some female domestic violence victims have been so brutalized by the men in their lives that a mere male presence may well terrify them. For that category of domestic violence victim, a women-only shelter may be the most compassionate and effective option.

(Men-only shelters for similarly devastated male victims would be equally valid.)

Nevertheless, it is difficult to understand why a male executive director who may have no direct interaction with battered women is so objectionable. To understand this response, it is necessary to enter the realm of ideology.

Judging an Entire Gender Guilty

The argument for a women-only space is rooted in a belief that domestic violence results from the general societal oppression of women as a class by men as a class.

The "Power and Control Wheel" that is used by every domestic violence organization I know of embodies this belief. The wheel explains the origins of domestic violence through a pie chart; one of the pie segments is labeled "Male Privilege."

In short, women-only feminists argue that women are battered not merely by an individual male abuser but by the entire male gender and, so, they must be protected from both.

This is similar to claiming that a white person who has been beaten by a black needs to be in a black-free environment because they have been battered not merely by a specific black person but by an entire race.

Women-only zealots are hurting victims.

To carry the analogy one step farther, it is similar to demanding that blacks should not be employed or allowed on the premises of a whites-only shelter . . . even if those premises are tax-funded and, so, prohibited from discrimination.

The ideological argument for women-only shelters—as opposed to the practical argument that, sometimes, such shelters just make sense—is class guilt. The guilty class is "male." Class guilt does not allow an individual male to demonstrate his innocence because, simply by being a member of a class, he is guilty by definition.

The concept of class guilt never ceases to anger me. As a victim of domestic violence, I know the fist that legally blinded my right eye was wielded by a specific man, not by a class. And I refuse to dilute his responsibility by extending it to men who've done me no harm.

It angers me as well because I'm the sort of domestic violence victim who needed exposure to non-abusive men, not isolation from all male presence, in order to heal. I needed to realize that decent caring men still existed and that I could interact with them in a positive way. In other words, a specific man was my problem; men as a whole were part of the solution.

Different Solutions for Different Styles of Healing

As I mentioned, there are domestic violence victims who do not share my reaction.

It would be amazing if hundreds of thousands of people—from different cultures, lifestyles and backgrounds—responded to a complex experience in exactly the same manner. Just as there is no one explanation for domestic violence, neither is there a one-size-fits-all remedy.

But the ideological women-only argument for domestic violence shelters is inflexible. It denies to female victims the healing presence of benevolent men with whom they can reestablish trust.

It denies the very possibility of male and female victims occupying the same shelter and, so, coming to an understanding of their differences and shared realities. Such mingling of the sexes is common in other forms of therapy and rehabilitation but it is akin to heresy to even suggest the prospect for domestic violence.

Denying Diversity, Harming Recovery

In short, women-only zealots dismiss the feminist goal of "diversity" and insist instead upon only one explanation for domestic violence and only one organizational principle for shelters.

Women-only zealots are hurting victims. They are harming those battered women who would benefit from learning how to regain their trust and respect for [men]. They are harming the significant percentage of domestic violence victims who are male themselves.

Estimates vary on the prevalence of male domestic violence victims. Professor Martin Fiebert of California State University at Long Beach prepared a summary of hundreds of studies and reports which indicates that men and women are victimized at much the same rate. A recent BOJ [Bureau of Justice Statistics] study found that men constituted 27 percent of domestic violence victims between 1998 and 2002.

Whichever figure is correct, a significant percentage of domestic violence victims are refused admission to most shelters in North America based solely upon their gender.

The anti-male prejudice in domestic violence must cease.

CHAPTER 4

What Is the Extent of Violence Against Women Worldwide?

Worldwide Violence Against Women: An Overview

United Nations Population Fund

The United Nations Population Fund is an international development agency that promotes the right of every woman, man, and child to enjoy a life of health and equal opportunity.

Violence against women and girls is a major human rights and public health concern.

It encompasses, a wide range of abuses [as reported by the United Nations General Assembly] from "physical, sexual and psychological violence occurring in the family and in the general community, including battering, sexual abuse of children, dowry-related violence, rape, female genital mutilation and other traditional practices harmful to women, non-spousal violence and violence related to exploitation, sexual harassment and intimidation at work, in educational institutions and elsewhere, trafficking in women, forced prostitution, and violence perpetrated or condoned by the state."

The Scope of the Problem

Domestic violence is the most common form of gender-based violence. In every country where reliable, large-scale studies have been conducted, between 10 and 69 per cent of women report they have been physically abused by an intimate partner in their lifetime.

Population-based studies report that from 12 to 25 per cent of women have experienced attempted or completed forced sex by an intimate partner or ex-partner at some time in their lives.

United Nations Population Fund, "Violence Against Women Fact Sheet," *State of the World Population 2005: Journalists' Press Kit*. Reproduced by permission of the United Nations Population Fund. 2005. http://www.unfpa.org/swp/2005/presskit/factsheets/facts_vaw.htm.

Studies on violence against women indicate that:

- The perpetrators of violence against women are almost exclusively men.

- Physical abuse in intimate relationships is almost always accompanied by severe psychological and verbal abuse. In 1 of 4 cases of domestic violence, women will also experience sexual abuse.

- Women are at greatest risk of violence from men they know. In Australia, Canada, Israel, South Africa and the United States, 40–70 per cent of female murder victims were killed by their partners.

Many men and women believe wife-beating is justified. The shame associated with domestic violence, rape and other forms of abuse may contribute to the fact that women often suffer it in silence, afraid of repercussions and stigma, and never tell anyone.

Gender-based violence burdens health care systems.

Other widespread forms of violence also have devastating impacts:

- Systematic rape, used as a weapon of war, has left millions of women and adolescent girls traumatized, forcibly impregnated, or infected with HIV.

- In Asia, at least 60 million girls are "missing" due to prenatal sex selection, infanticide or neglect.

- Female genital mutilation/cutting affects an estimated 130 million women and girls. Each year, 2 million more undergo the practice. Violence against women also takes the form of other harmful practices—such as child marriage, honour killings, acid burning, dowry-related violence, and widow inheritance and cleansing (both of which increase HIV risks).

Forced prostitution, trafficking for sex and sex tourism appear to be growing problems. Each year, an estimated 800,000 people are trafficked across borders—80 per cent of them women and girls. Most of them end up trapped in the commercial sex trade. This figure does not include the substantial number of women and girls who are bought and sold within their own countries, for which there are scant data.

Reports of trafficking in women come from nearly every world region. The greatest number of victims are believed to come from Asia (about 250,000 per year), the former Soviet Union (about 100,000), and from Central and Eastern Europe (about 175,000). An estimated 100,000 trafficked women have come from Latin America and the Caribbean, with more than 50,000 from Africa. War, displacement, and economic and social inequities between and within countries, and the demand for low-wage labour and sex work drive this illicit trade in women.

Health, Societal and Economic Impact

Abused women are more likely than others to suffer from depression, anxiety, psychosomatic symptoms, eating problems, sexual dysfunction and many reproductive health problems, including miscarriage and stillbirth, premature delivery, HIV and other sexually transmitted infections, unwanted pregnancies and unsafe abortions.

Consequences of abuse, such as HIV/AIDS or unplanned pregnancies, may in themselves act as risk factors for further aggression, forming a cycle of abuse. Adolescents who have experienced sexual abuse are more likely to experience it again later in life.

About 1 in 4 women are abused during pregnancy, which puts both mother and child at risk.

Gender-based violence burdens health care systems: Studies from Nicaragua, the United States and Zimbabwe indicate that women who have been physically or sexually assaulted use health services more than women with no history of violence.

Violence against women represents a drain on the economically productive workforce: Canada's national survey on violence against women reported that 30 per cent of battered wives had to cease regular activities due to the abuse, and 50 per cent of women had to take sick leave from work because of the harm sustained.

Violence against women has high costs in terms of national expenditures on health, courts and police, as well as losses in educational achievement and productivity. In the United States, intimate partner violence is estimated to cost some $12.6 billion a year. In India, a survey showed that for each incidence of violence, women lost an average of 7 working days.

A study of abused women in Managua, Nicaragua, found that abused women earned 46 per cent less than women who did not suffer abuse, even after controlling for other factors that affect earnings.

Violence Against Women Is Often Used as a Weapon of War

Amnesty International

Amnesty International is a worldwide organization that campaigns for internationally recognized human rights to be respected and protected.

They took K.M., who is 12 years old, in the open air. Her father was killed by the Janjawid in Um Baru, the rest of the family ran away and she was captured by the Janjawid who were on horseback. More than six people used her as a wife; she stayed with the Janjawid and the military more than 10 days. K., another woman who is married, aged 18, ran away but was captured by the Janjawid who slept with her in the open place, all of them slept with her. She is still with them. A., a teacher, told me that they broke her leg after raping her.

A 66-year-old farmer from Um Baru
in the district of Kutum, Darfur, western Sudan.

As conflict escalated in late 2003 and early 2004 in Darfur region, western Sudan, Amnesty International began to receive hundreds of reports of rape and other sexual violence against women and girls. It also emerged that women and girls were being abducted to be used as sex slaves or domestic workers.

Most of the perpetrators were members of the government-backed armed militia, the *Janjawid*, but mounting evidence indicated that government soldiers were also involved. Even women who reached refugee camps were not safe. In March 2004 alone, the UN [United Nations] was told that in the camp for internally displaced persons in Mornei, western Dar-

Amnesty International, *Lives Blown Apart: Crimes Against Women in Times of Conflict: Stop Violence Against Women*, London: Amnesty International, 2004. Copyright © 2004 Amnesty International Publications. All rights reserved. Reproduced by permission.

fur, up to 16 women were being raped every day as they went to collect water. The women had to go to the river—their families needed the water and they feared that the men would be killed if they went instead.

Conflict reinforces and exacerbates existing patterns of discrimination and violence against women.

The horrific pattern of sexual and other violence against women which has emerged from Darfur is by no means unique. In recent years, hundreds of thousands of women affected by conflict around the world have suffered the same fate. In the recent conflict in the Democratic Republic of Congo (DRC), tens of thousands of women and girls have been raped. In Colombia widespread sexual violence is an integral part of the armed conflict and is committed by all sides—the security forces, army-backed paramilitaries and guerrilla forces. Lesser known conflicts such as that in the Solomon Islands have also left a legacy of violence against women: in the first six months of 2004 alone, 200 women reported to the Solomon Islands police that they had been raped.

This report attempts to explore some of the underlying reasons for this violence. Evidence gathered by Amnesty International in recent years supports the view that conflict reinforces and exacerbates existing patterns of discrimination and violence against women. The violence women suffer in conflict is an extreme manifestation of the discrimination and abuse women face in peacetime, and the unequal power relations between men and women in most societies. In peacetime, such attitudes contribute to the widespread acceptance of domestic violence, rape and other forms of sexual abuse against women. When political tensions and increasing militarization spill over into outright conflict, these habitual attitudes and abuses take on new dimensions and distinctive patterns, and all forms of violence increase, including rape and other forms of sexual violence against women.

A Broad Spectrum of Violence Against Women

Although the UN Security Council has recently recognized that "civilians, particularly women and children, account for the vast majority of those adversely affected by armed conflict, including as refugees and internally displaced persons, and increasingly are targeted by combatants and armed elements", there is still a widespread perception that women play only a secondary or peripheral role in situations of conflict.

Women of a particular community or social group may be assaulted because they are seen as embodying the 'honour' and integrity of the community.

This report describes the use by states and armed groups of gender-based violence in conflict. The use of rape as a weapon of war is perhaps the most notorious and brutal way in which conflict impacts on women. As rape and sexual violence are so pervasive within situations of conflict, the "rape victim" has become an emblematic image of women's experience of war.

This report seeks to show the many other ways in which women and girls are targeted for violence, or otherwise affected by war, in disproportionate or different ways from men. The report highlights how the many roles which women play in conflict, and the variety of contexts they find themselves in, can have a devastating impact on their physical integrity and basic rights. This report also refers to the broader phenomenon of militarization which often precedes conflict, which almost always accompanies it, and which can remain as part of its legacy. For the purposes of this report, militarization is the process whereby military values, institutions and patterns of behaviour have an increasingly dominant influence over society.

Vulnerable Civilians

Women are likely to be among the primary victims of direct attacks on the civilian population, as they usually constitute the majority of the non-combatant population. They also generally bear the brunt of so-called "collateral damage"—the killing or maiming of civilians as a result of military attacks. Even so-called "precision bombing" exacts a heavy civilian toll, while landmines and unexploded ordnance do not distinguish between military and civilian footsteps. Domestic work, social restrictions on their mobility and other factors may mean that women are often less able to flee when the civilian population comes under attack.

Damage to the economic infrastructure and environment raises particular problems for women in societies where they have primary responsibility for providing food and water for their families.

Individual women may be specifically targeted for torture or for killings because they are community leaders, because they have challenged social mores about appropriate roles for women, or because of the activities of their male relatives. Women are targeted as peace activists, as mediators and negotiators in conflict and as human rights defenders and humanitarian aid workers. Many of these abuses take gender-specific forms.

If detained or imprisoned, women may be held in inappropriate detention facilities and will often be at risk of gender-based torture, including rape and other forms of sexual abuse, by their jailors or fellow inmates.

In situations of inter-communal strife or conflicts drawn along ethnic or religious lines, women of a particular community or social group may be assaulted because they are seen as embodying the "honour" and integrity of the community.

Women and children form the majority of the millions of refugees and displaced people fleeing situations of conflict, exposing them to privations of many kinds and to further risk of sexual violence. It has been estimated that 80 per cent of refugees are women and children. Yet refugee camps are often planned and administered in such a way that women living there face discrimination and continued risk of sexual abuse.

The trafficking of women and girls for sexual exploitation and forced labour has been a common characteristic of conflicts and post-conflict situations throughout history. In recent years, UN and other peacekeeping forces, as well as humanitarian aid workers, have been implicated in trafficking.

In many parts of the world, more and more women and girls are becoming combatants, whether voluntarily or by coercion, in both regular armies and armed groups. Some are recruited into armed groups for the purpose of sexual exploitation or are subjected to sexual violence as part of "initiation" rituals. Some also become perpetrators, responsible for human rights abuses. Many other women may be forced to contribute to the war effort in other ways, such as preparing munitions, uniforms and other military equipment.

Economic, Social, and Cultural Violence Against Women

The increasing international focus on sexual violence committed in the context of conflict, while necessary and important, has tended to obscure other important aspects of women's experience of conflict and militarization. These include the disproportionate and differential impact of conflict on their economic, social and cultural rights, including their right to health.

The role that women are expected to play as carers and guardians of the family can cause them to be particularly hard hit, both financially and emotionally, by the loss of family members or the destruction of their homes. In conflict situations, many women must take on additional roles as sole heads of household providing for their families. Damage to the economic infrastructure and environment raises particular problems for women in societies where they have primary responsibility for providing food and water for their families. The many women around the world who depend on subsistence agriculture face the risk of crossfire, landmines or forcible eviction. Grazing cattle, tending fields, taking produce to market or collecting water or firewood may prove impossible. War widows have to raise their children while trying to eke out a living in difficult circumstances.

Some of the worst atrocities against women have been committed by 'non-state actors,' in particular by armed groups.

The damage caused by conflict often means that women no longer have access to healthcare appropriate to their needs, whether in their communities, in camps for refugees and displaced people, in prisons, barracks or camps used by combatants, or in demobilization camps established in the aftermath of conflict. When primary healthcare services collapse completely in the context of conflict, women are affected differently, and often disproportionately, because of their distinct health needs and care responsibilities.

In most conflicts, women remain largely absent from peace-making, peacekeeping and peace-building initiatives, even those backed by the international community. In the aftermath of hostilities, disarmament, demobilization, rehabilitation and reintegration programmes may not cater for their needs or match their experiences.

Violence can take a variety of different forms, psychological as well as physical, resulting in extreme economic hardship and social deprivation which deny women economic, social and cultural rights, as well as their civil and political rights. Even where women suffer the same human rights violations as men, these may have different consequences for women. Women often face particular barriers to access to justice and redress, and endure social stigma in post-conflict societies because of the abuses they have suffered.

Those who carry out the abuses are many and varied: soldiers of the state's armed forces; pro-government paramilitary groups or militias; armed groups fighting the government or at war with other armed groups; the police, prison guards or private security and military personnel; military forces stationed abroad, including UN and other peacekeeping forces; staff of humanitarian agencies; neighbours and relatives. Places where such violence occurs are equally diverse: detention centres, displaced persons and refugee camps, at checkpoints and border crossings, in public places, in the community and in the home. . . .

Conflict and Security in the 21st Century

Military aggression, foreign occupation, failed or collapsed states, inter-communal tensions or conflicts generated by competition for resources are an ongoing reality affecting people across the globe. The number of conflicts shows no signs of waning. Between 1989 and 1997 for example, there were an estimated 103 armed conflicts in 69 countries. In Africa alone, over one quarter of the continent's 53 countries suffered conflicts in the late 1990s. And in this world at war, the victims are increasingly civilians, most of whom are non-combatant women and children.

A common characteristic of many conflicts at the start of the 21st century is the exploitation of perceived racial, ethnic, religious, cultural or political differences in order to set community against community. In such contexts, sexual violence is particularly likely to be used as a weapon of war. Women of a particular racial, ethnic or religious group may be targeted for violence aimed at their sexual integrity and reproductive capacity, as the perceived bearers of the community's cultural identity and the reproducers of their society.

Few of today's wars are international conflicts fought exclusively between professional national armies. Although international tensions continue in numerous parts of the world, the majority of conflicts are internal conflicts between governments and armed groups, or between several competing armed groups. Some of the worst atrocities against women have been committed by "non-state actors", in particular by armed groups. Holding those responsible to account can be a formidable challenge. The chain-of-command structure of such groups may be difficult to establish. They may not recognize any obligations under international humanitarian law. Judicial mechanisms for bringing the perpetrators to justice in accordance with fair trial standards may not exist, particularly in areas under armed group control.

The devastating attacks on 11 September 2001 highlighted a new type of threat from armed groups. While acts of terror against civilians are nothing new, attacks such as those in Nairobi, New York, Bali, Casablanca, Madrid and Beslan shocked the conscience of people worldwide because of their scale and deliberate cruelty. The fact that many of today's armed groups operate in loose international networks using such tactics as suicide bombing makes it all the more difficult to track down those responsible and prevent future attacks.

Harming Women in the Name of Security

The new global security environment since 11 September 2001 has led to abuses by governments in the context of the US-led "war on terror". New doctrines of security have stretched the concept of "war" into areas formerly considered law enforcement, promoting the notion that human rights can be curtailed when it comes to the detention, interrogation and prosecution of "terrorist" suspects.

The new security environment has also led to some countries imposing greater restrictions on immigrants and asylum-seekers, many of them women who have fled conflict or who sought to work and send funds back to family members in war-torn countries. For example, the effect of procedural delays and limitations imposed by the US government after 11 September 2001 led to a sharp fall in the number of foreigners who became permanent US immigrants in 2003. Increased restrictions on would-be refugees, migrant workers or immigrants have also been reported from other countries including Japan, where restrictions are likely to impact particularly on women domestic workers seeking employment there.

The US-led military intervention in Iraq has heightened concerns that the world may be entering a new era of preventive or pre-emptive wars, where military force may be used in disregard of the restrictions contained in the UN Charter. Given the prominent position of the USA on the world stage, US policy will to a great extent determine future trends regarding militarization, the use of force and the conduct of armed conflict.

Another characteristic of contemporary conflict is the role of powerful economic interests in fanning the flames and reaping the profits of conflict and militarization. If more conflicts are fought over natural resources in future, the role of corporate actors will be all the more significant and decisive. Just as women's experiences can no longer be overlooked in policy debates around security, so urgent attention will need to be paid to the economic and social dimensions of human security if future conflicts are to be averted.

Today, there can no longer be any excuse for ignoring the scale of crimes against women in conflict. With almost daily news reports from war zones across the globe, no one can claim that they do not know what is happening. Nor can one hide behind the excuse that nothing can be done. There is an urgent need to find more effective forms of action proportionate to the scale and gravity of the crimes that are unfolding.

Femicide Is a Serious Problem in East Asia

Andrea Parrot and Nina Cummings

Andrea Parrot is a professor in the Department of Policy Analysis and Management at Cornell University in New York and is the author of numerous publications about women's issues. Nina Cummings is a health educator at Cornell University specializing in women's health who uses her expertise in domestic violence and sexual violence prevention in her capacity as the university victim advocate.

This [viewpoint] examines the disproportionate killing of female fetuses (feticide) and infant girls (infanticide) that results in a significant gender imbalance in favor of males. These practices are not the only factors that account for such a gender imbalance in countries where it is practiced; trafficking, wife and intimate partner murder, sexual slavery, and the selling of female children also contribute to the significantly fewer girls and women in the population.

Infanticide and feticide have been used as the means to eliminate unwanted children throughout history, however these practices have been and still are disproportionately applied to females. . . . Female infanticide and feticide most commonly occur in Asia; as such, China and India are a focus [in this viewpoint.]

Favoring Sons

Males tend to be most highly prized in countries where females leave their parents and move into their husbands' homes with the husbands' parents when they marry. The circumstances then make married women unavailable to care for their parents as they age, and the parents of only girls face old age without caretakers. The bride's labor and availability are transferred to her husband's family upon marriage, leaving her parents with limited or no assistance. This system is present in both India and China.

Motherhood has been exalted and venerated, but in many parts of the world this is contingent upon whether the mother gives birth to sons.

Sons are preferred because in addition to being wage earners, they can also bring other economic assets to the extended family in the form of dowry or the unpaid labor of the wife. There are many societies in which only males can carry out religious, social, familial, or cultural responsibilities. Not only are females unable to do most of these things, they are also often a financial burden on a family as in the case of dowry, where girls are expected to marry and provide substantial sums of money and gifts to her husband's family.

Motherhood has been exalted and venerated, but in many parts of the world this is contingent upon whether the mother gives birth to sons; women are often viewed as nothing more than wombs to bear sons. In India, for example, only sons carry on the family name, and according to Hindu tradition, only a son can light his parents funeral pyre thereby assuring their safe passage to the afterlife. A son is believed to be more of an economic asset through wage earning and by attracting a substantial dowry. [According to psychologist Vikran Patel] this attitude "manifests itself in the systematic neglect of girl children when it comes to breast feeding, nurturing, food intake, health care, personality development, property rights, and in extreme cases female infanticide." One of the long-term consequences of infanticide and feticide is a shortage of brides for men of marrying age. In South Korea the difference between males and females of reproductive age is projected to be 940,000. Projecting further to the year 2020, in China there will be 35 million more males than females; in India, 25 million; and in Pakistan, 4 million.

> I lay on my bed weak after childbirth. My mother-in-law picked up the baby and started feeding her milk. I knew what she was doing. I cried and tried to stop her. But she had already given her milk laced with yerakkam paal [the poisonous juice of the oleander plant]. Within minutes, "the baby turned blue and died," Karuppayee says matter-of-factly.

The two mechanisms typically employed to support cultural male preference are infanticide and feticide.

Birth Rates and Gender

In 1994, 117 boys were born for every 100 girls in China. By 2002, that ratio was 109 boys for every 100 girls. Some governmental and cultural attempts to stop the femicide have been showing promise. However, relying primarily on laws has only reduced the problem, not eliminated it. The cultural norms that drive these practices must also be addressed and challenged. In China, as well as other countries where males are more highly valued, the ratio of males to females is significantly higher, especially if couples are permitted only one child. The phenomenon of missing girls in China in the 1980s was documented to have been related to the government's population policies, such as the one-child policy. In Korea in 1995, the male to female sex ratio under the age of five was 108.5, with higher ratios of males in large cities such as Taegu and Pusan. As of 2002 in South Korea there were 111 boys per 100 girls and in India, 105 boys to every 100 girls born. In India, by adulthood, the ratio shifts to 107 males for every 100 females. Because sex-selective abortions and prenatal diagnostic tests for sex determination are illegal and under tight surveillance in India, some mothers who might have aborted their fetuses are carrying them to term. However, when unwanted girls are born, systemic neglect of health and nutrition of females and high rates of maternal mortality and abuse in adulthood continue to decrease the numbers of girls and women. With natural disasters such as the 2004 tsunami when food and clean water are scarce, one wonders if the limited resources will be distributed equally to male and female children. If male children are disproportionately given access to the resources, this may lead to an even greater gender imbalance in the areas affected by natural disasters.

Types of Femicide

The two mechanisms typically employed to support cultural male preference are infanticide and feticide. There are other manifestations of this preference, such as neglect or lack of medical treatment of older female children. However, sex-selective killing of females on the largest scale occurs before or shortly after birth. While most countries have a sex ratio of approximately 104 boy babies born to every 100 girl babies, the countries highlighted in this [viewpoint] have sex ratios at birth of 110 to 100. In other countries where infanticide is the primary method of femicide, the ratio at birth is similar to the worldwide average but changes in favor of males shortly after. In the normal course of events, the ratio ultimately increases in favor of females due to a variety of reasons: males die younger and more often due to injuries, wars, and so on.

Infanticide is a reflection of the deadly consequences for females of the cultural domination of patriarchal cultural values.

Infanticide

Infanticide is the deliberate killing of a child in its infancy, including death through neglect. Historically it has been practiced on every continent, and the gender of the infant killed is almost always preferentially female, especially in periods of famine and poverty. Female infanticide has been practiced in such diverse cultures as Ancient Rome, among the Yanomami Indians of Brazil, and in Arabian tribes.

The countries currently with a sex ratio imbalance due to infanticide or sex selective abortions include India, China, Guam, Pakistan, Taiwan, Hong Kong, and the Republic of South Korea. In some instances infanticide and feticide are employed; in others where there are no restrictions on the number of children, parents may continue to produce children until they have fewer daughters than sons. In large and diverse countries such as China and India, these practices are not universally employed but tend to be more common in the rural regions. The inner-land provinces of China are, in general, more isolated from outside influences and are subject to greater poverty, have greater need in physical labors, and preserve more traditional gendered ideologies compared with the coastal areas.

Because there are almost no examples of groups engaging in preferential male infanticide as a universal social practice, infanticide is a reflection of the deadly consequences for females of the cultural domination of patriarchal cultural values. This practice represents a crime of gender in the form of persistent and extreme abuse and devaluation of females and reflects the authoritarian and hierarchal assumption that the male engendered version of the "natural order" of the world is legitimate. Justifications for infanticide are economic, familial, and societal. Medical testing for sex selection, though officially outlawed, has become a booming business in China, India, and the Republic of Korea. Though no reliable infanticide statistics are available because many, perhaps most, cases are unreported, substantial disparities in gender population figures in these areas remain. "[According to researcher S. Hom,] the killing of infant girls is a form of violence against the infant herself, the mother, and all women in the society in which the practice occurs. Female infanticide is a gender-based discriminatory judgment about who will survive."

Some parents are choosing sex determination and abortion over infanticide for which they are less likely to be arrested.

Blaming the Mother

Because women are blamed for the sex of their children, women who have given birth to girls . . . "have been poisoned, strangled, bludgeoned, and socially ostracized . . . [some have been driven] to suicide, others into mental institutions. . . . The pressure on women is so great that many openly weep on learning that they have given birth to a girl." Women who are abused in India frequently experience this violence because they have given birth to a girl or for failing to give birth to a boy. This attitude is misguided. Because the male's sperm determines the sex of the fetus, to prevent women from being blamed for giving birth to daughters, one strategy may be to clarify and emphasize the father's role in determining the sex of the child. When mothers make the decision to kill their babies, one wonders if they do so for themselves, their babies, or both. African women onboard slave ships crossing the Atlantic during the sixteenth and seventeenth centuries killed their children because they were demoralized and desperate about being enslaved and wanted their child to be in a better place. Slave women in the United States were driven to infanticide, often after they were raped, to save their infant girls from the lives of misery that they themselves were forced to endure. Women who kill their infant girls sometimes do so to keep them from experiencing the torture that they believe awaits their daughters within their culture: harassment, battering, alcoholism of their husbands, sexual abuse, shame, humiliation, and loss of dignity.

Feticide

In some countries, such as China, infanticide is being replaced by feticide (abortion of female fetuses), now that ultrasound can determine the sex of a fetus with a high degree of certainty. High tech medical tests to visualize the fetus in utero (ultrasound scans) or to determine the gender of the fetus through genetic testing early in pregnancy, such as amniocentesis and chorionic villi biopsies (CVB), are being used to support the elimination of unwanted female fetuses. These medical techniques are more readily accessible because of improved mobility between rural and urban areas. Amniocentesis can be extremely accurate for determining sex at about sixteen weeks, while CVB is reliable at approximately twelve weeks. Some parents are choosing sex determination and abortion over infanticide for which they are less likely to be arrested. Because feticide is the interruption of development of a fetus that parents haven't seen, it may be less traumatic than killing a newborn baby.

Because of the double bind women are in, laws that target the individual woman who kills her daughter will not stop infanticide.

Ultrasound is used most frequently in India and China because it is the more accessible and the least invasive and expensive of the three. Ultrasound is also less definitive than the other two and often will not yield the necessary information as early as the more invasive tests. A sex determination (SD) ultrasound scan can cost more than 300 rupees in India. The ultrasound and an abortion may cost as much as 7,000 rupees. But many families can't afford ultrasound and abortion. Although infanticide is illegal, while abortion is not, it is cheaper to kill a baby girl after it is born. Among the Bihari in India, a common sentiment is that "it is better to be aborted than burned by one's mother-in-law after marriage for insufficient dowry." Bride burning, which often results in death, occurs when the bride's dowry is considered insufficient by her in-laws.

Health care practitioners in India are engaged in debate over the appropriateness of SD tests. Some support SD as a population control measure. Others respect the choice of the couple and perform the test to help the woman prevent beatings by her husband and other family members for producing a daughter. A third point of view supports SD tests to identify fetal abnormalities only. Some oppose SD tests because they are opposed to abortion. . . .

The Pressure to Commit Femicide

Most laws to stop female infanticide criminalize women responsible for the killing, usually the mother, grandmother, or midwife. But cultural discrimination and individual-directed blame create an environment that forces women to perpetrate these crimes. Women are blamed for giving birth to girls and are punished for it as well. To avoid the blame and punishment, they are under unimaginable pressure to sacrifice their daughters. It is the equivalent of social infanticide. Understanding that this is social, rather than individual infanticide, policymakers and leaders at the institutional and ideological levels have a responsibility to challenge the underlying assumptions that allow infanticide to be an available option to women oppressed by the conditions in which they live. Because of the double bind women are in, laws that target the individual woman who kills her daughter will not stop infanticide. Social reform is essential if there is to be any meaningful reduction in the practice.

The cultural scripts a woman lives with, combined with the obligations to her family, and socialization to subordinate her own needs to the men in her life all contribute to infanticide and feticide. Although many women live with poverty, neglect, and subordination, they are held accountable for the violence in their lives. Objectified, with the main purpose of creating more males, they are declared murderers when the system forces them to carry out patriarchal and misogynistic ideals. In addition to other forms of oppression, such as race and class, female infanticide constitutes a deadly denial of women's rights to life and liberty on a large scale. It is one of the more insidious of the many manifestations of violence against women.

Crimes of "Honour" Are a Serious Problem in the Middle East

United Nations

The United Nations and its family of organizations work to promote respect for human rights, protect the environment, fight disease, and reduce poverty around the globe.

A young Bangladeshi woman was flogged to death by order of village clerics for "immoral behaviour". An Egyptian man paraded the head of his daughter on a stick through the streets of his neighbourhood after he killed her for besmirching his name. A teenager's throat was slit in Turkey because a love ballad was dedicated to her over the radio. A Pakistani woman was gunned down by her own family in the presence of her human rights lawyer for pursuing a divorce from her abusive husband. A 13-year-old Turkish girl's husband slit her throat in a public square after pulling her out of a cinema and accusing her of being a prostitute. A 35-year-old Jordanian man shot and killed his sister for reporting to the police that she had been raped. A Turkish girl was killed by her father for telling the authorities that she had been raped and then refusing his demand that she marry the rapist. A 29-year-old woman was dragged from her house in Afghanistan by her husband and local officials and stoned to death for committing adultery, while the man with whom she was alleged to have had an affair was whipped and then freed.

A Culturally Condoned Atrocity

Each of these executions was committed within the past five years [2000–2005] in the name of "honour". Many of the perpetrators received no criminal penalties, others served only short sentences. Considered justifiable punishment for a wide range of perceived offences, contemporary honour crimes are based on archaic codes of social conduct that severely circumscribe female behaviour while at the same time legitimising male violence against women.

Honour crimes are typically engineered by male family members but are often tacitly or explicitly condoned by the community and/or the state. In many countries the responsibility for the murder itself is assigned to an underage male, thus ensuring a (reduced) juvenile sentence in the event the case is prosecuted. In most instances, the murderer is hailed as a "true man". It is also not unheard of for female family members to act as accomplices to the killing or even to carry out the murder itself.

The Scale of the Problem

In recent reports, both the United Nations Special Rapporteur for Violence Against Women and the Special Rapporteur for Extrajudicial and Summary Executions have highlighted this egregious type of violence against women, citing incidents in Bangladesh, Turkey, Jordan, Israel, India, Italy, Pakistan, Brazil, Ecuador, Uganda, Morocco, Syria, Egypt, Lebanon, Iran and Yemen, as well as among migrant communities in Germany, France, Sweden and the United Kingdom. Honour crimes also have been reported in Afghanistan and Iraq.

What masquerades as honour is really men's need to control women's sexuality and freedom.

The actual scale of the problem is impossible to determine. In many cases deaths are not registered; in others murders are made to look like suicides, or women are forced or induced by their families to kill themselves. Burns or acid attacks not resulting in death often are attributed to accidents, a claim which victims may not refute for fear of further reprisals. In societies where these crimes occur, protection and support are often extended to the perpetrator rather than to the victim.

Despite the lack of reliable statistical data, estimates based on reviews of police reports and court dockets, newspaper articles and other sources in a variety of countries suggest that thousands of women and girls are murdered each year in the name of honour. Anecdotal evidence from Pakistan, for example, suggests that more than 1,000 women are victims of honour crimes annually. Over one-third of femicides in Jordan are thought to be such killings. In Turkey, an annual report of the Human Rights Association concluded that more than half of women killed by family members in 2003 were victims of honour crimes.

In 1997, the former attorney general of the Palestinian National Authority suggested that 70 percent of all murders of women in Gaza and the West Bank were honour crimes. In the same year, as many as 400 honour killings took place in Yemen, and 57 were reported in Egypt. In late 2004, 117 murders in the United Kingdom were being investigated as possible honour killings. In Lebanon, 36 honour crimes were reported between 1996 and 1998.

According to the Special Rapporteur on Violence Against Women, the number of honour killings "is on the rise as the perception of what constitutes honour and what damages it widens." Its global prevalence suggests that honour crimes are not unique to specific cultures, religions or classes. In fact, the justification for these crimes has it roots in various social and legal systems around the world.

Women as Property

In the broadest sense, honour crimes involve the murder or maiming of a woman or girl whose behaviour is at odds (whether in fact or by perception) with the norms of the society in which she lives. In many cases the cause of the woman's actions—even if she is under extreme duress or in fear of her life—is immaterial if her family feels that she has compromised their supposed honour. The inherent subjectivity of such notions of honour opens these codes to wide and convenient interpretation. At the most basic level, "what masquerades as honour is really men's need to control women's sexuality and freedom," [according to the Special Rapporteur].

Some experts believe that honour crimes also are used to cover up misdeeds such as rape, incest, adultery, unlawful or undesired pregnancies and for inheritance purposes.

According to Thaira Shahid Khan, the author of *Chained to Custom*, "Women are considered the property of the males and their family irrespective of their class, ethnic or religious group. The owner of the property has the right to decide its fate. The concept of ownership has turned women into a commodity which can be exchanged, bought and sold." That perception also means that women are expendable when their actions, real or imagined, threaten a family's sense of honour.

Justification for Honour Crimes

While honour crimes are most prevalent in Muslim and some Mediterranean cultures, the popular conflation of Islam with such acts is misguided: Islamic scholars and clerics alike have publicly decried the practice, confirming that it has no basis in Islamic scripture or teachings. Nevertheless, in traditional Muslim societies, concerns about shame and honour may take precedence over individual human rights and freedoms. One contention is that honour crimes have their origins in the Arabic expression "A man's honour lies between the legs of a woman." In Turkish, the term *namus* is used to describe honour. A woman's *namus* is primarily defined through her sexuality, her physical appearance and her behaviour, a man's *namus* is achieved through the sexual purity of his wife, daughters or sisters.

Others contend that current justifications for crimes of honour are the result of colonial influences, including both Napoleonic and British codes that cite provocation as an exonerating or mitigating factor in criminal assault. Indeed, the concept of provocation in "crimes of passion" between men and women—where women are held accountable for inciting men to violence—has tenacious roots in many societies across the world. As recently as 1999, an American man was sentenced to only four months in prison for murdering his wife and wounding her lover in the presence of their 10-year-old son.

In Sindh, Pakistan, honour crimes take the form of *karo-kari* killings. *Karo* literally means a "black man" and *kari* means a "black woman". Having brought dishonour to their families through adultery or other "inappropriate" behaviour, the customary punishment for both *karo* and *kari* is death. In practice, however, the *kari* woman is usually killed first, giving the *karo* man an opportunity to flee. Following the woman's punishment, the man may be able to negotiate a truce with the dishonoured family by paying financial compensation and/or by replacing the woman who was killed with a woman from his own family.

In some instances, reputed *karo-kari* killings can serve as pretence for economic gain. In fact, evidence suggests that faked honour killings often conceal other crimes: Men murder other men for reasons not associated with honour and then execute a woman of their own family to camouflage the initial killing. Some experts believe that honour crimes also are used to cover up misdeeds such as rape, incest, adultery, unlawful or undesired pregnancies and for inheritance purposes. In Jordan, for example, investigators surmise that a substantial portion of the 20 to 35 honour killings documented each year are the result of other motives.

An Ever-Present Threat

In settings where honour killings are prevalent, the constant threat against women and girls is yet another form of violence, aptly described in the Pakistani poet Attiya Dawood's rendering of the daily experience of a young Pakistani girl: "My brother's eyes forever follow me. My father's gaze guards me all the time, stern, angry . . . We stand accused and condemned to be declared *kari* and murdered."

Police rarely investigate honour crimes, and the handful of perpetrators who are arrested often receive only token punishments.

For some women, this threat leads to suicide, whether or not a family orders it. One young woman in Pakistan, for example, laid herself across a train track after being pressured by her parents to marry a man she did not choose. Other women and girls may be forced to undergo virginity exams—an often painful and degrading process—and are still killed despite medical verification of their chastity.

Little Punishment of Perpetrators

Whether or not the threat of violence actually results in murder, the risk of being killed results in the virtual death of many women, whose only option, in the absence of adequate protective services, is to enter prisons or other custodial facilities. In Jordan, for example, police imprison potential victims to protect them from being killed by their male relatives. While those who threaten them remain free, victims languish in custody for years on end. In some societies, women are not released from custody until a relative signs for their discharge. Too often, a woman or girl who is handed over to relatives who promise to protect her is immediately killed by them. In one instance, Jordanian police returned a 36-year-old woman to her father's home after he had consented not to hurt her. He shot her while the police were still downstairs, and his punishment was one month in prison.

Evidence suggests that there is a great demand for services, including shelters, for abused women. But even where shelters are available, there is often little they can provide in terms of concrete assistance because of the limited rights and opportunities afforded to women by the prevailing culture. Moreover, shelter workers, human rights activists, journalists and lawyers are at risk of being targeted by angry families and communities.

Police rarely investigate honour crimes, and the handful of perpetrators who are arrested often receive only token punishments. In some settings police may overtly or covertly champion the killers as vindicated men. Elsewhere, police act within a network of conspirators who benefit economically from honour killings. Many countries where such crimes are commonplace have retained legislation allowing reduced sentences or exemption from prosecution for those who commit honour crimes.

Education programmes in some local communities about the tenets of Islam that proscribe honour crimes have been valuable in mobilising against the practice.

In Pakistan, for example, an ordinance gives the heirs of a murder victim the right to pardon the murderer. Since family members most often are complicit in honour killings, many perpetrators go free. Specific articles in the Jordanian penal code offer similar protection. In Brazil, men alleging adultery may also go free. In one such case, a man stabbed his wife and her lover to death after catching them in a hotel room. The case was appealed three times, and each time the jury acquitted the defendant. Such defences are found to varying degrees in the penal codes of Peru, Bangladesh, Argentina, Ecuador, Egypt, Guatemala, Iran, Israel, Syria, Lebanon, Turkey, the West Bank and Venezuela.

Taking Action Against Honour Crimes

The work of local and international activists is bringing gradual pressure to bear in many of the countries where honour crimes are most prevalent. Turkey, for example, has taken steps to conform its legislation to international standards. In 2003 and 2004, three defendants were sentenced to life imprisonment for crimes of honour. Real change, however, takes time. In another case in 2004, the 24-year sentence of a man convicted of killing his wife was commuted to two years after he presented to the court pictures of his wife with another man. In Pakistan, intensive pressure on the government has resulted in the drafting of legislation against honour crimes, which has yet to be formally presented to parliament.

A grassroots campaign against honour killing in Jordan gathered some 15,000 signatures on a petition to repeal an article in the penal code that pardons honour crimes that are the result of a wife committing adultery. In 2001, a temporary amendment was passed precluding exoneration based on adultery, although it retained adultery as a mitigating circumstance. To date [2005], ratification of the amendment is still pending, and parliamentary resistance to the legislation is apparently strong in some conservative quarters.

One Jordanian member of parliament who opposed repealing the law on honour crimes opined, "Women adulterers cause a great threat to our society because they are the main reasons that such acts take place. . . . If men do not find women with whom to commit adultery, then they will become good on their own."

There are differing opinions about the best ways to address the problem of honour crimes. Some argue that any local efforts must be supported by the international community, while others express concern that intensive media coverage by the international press—Western press, in particular—may generate a backlash that undermines the important work of local activists. Similarly, education programmes in some local communities about the tenets of Islam that proscribe honour crimes have been valuable in mobilising against the practice. Project workers elsewhere, however, have found that invoking the Qur'an has not proven useful in denouncing violence. They favour promoting traditional preventive practices of family dialogue to support mediation and reconciliation.

Changing Laws and Culture Perspectives

Most parties agree, however, that eradication strategies must support the implementation of protective laws. Tunisia is an example where legislative reform has had considerable success. Historically, several provisions in Tunisian law reduced criminal penalties for perpetrators of honour killings. Derived from the Napoleonic code and influenced by colonial history, these provisions held wives, but not husbands, criminally liable for adulterous behaviour and stipulated significantly reduced penalties for murderous husbands who caught their wives in an act of adultery. Reforms in both these provisions were accomplished in the last three decades with little debate or dissent from the Muslim leaders or populace. Notably, there have been no documented cases of honour crimes in Tunisia in the last twenty years.

Most activists also agree that efforts must be vastly but incrementally increased to promote shifts in community perceptions about gender roles, rights and responsibilities. Such initiatives may be slow-paced, but the goals are nonetheless radical: "In the end, honour killings will only be eradicated when power over women is not seen as central to a man's self-respect, and domination of women and girls is not seen as reassuring social glue." At that point, there will be no more "honour" in killing wives, sisters and mothers.

Female Genital Mutilation Is a Serious Problem

Feminist Majority Foundation

Founded in 1987, the Feminist Majority Foundation advocates for the legal, social, and political equality of women with men and trains young feminists to be leaders in the feminist movement in the United States.

Female genital mutilation (FGM), sometimes called female genital cutting (FGC) or female circumcision, is the cutting or removal of all or a portion of the female genitals for cultural (not medical) reasons. There are different ways it is practiced according to the place or culture in which it is being done. The World Health Organization describes them in the following types:

Type I (Clitoridectomy): removal of part or all of the clitoris.

Type II (Excision): This is the most common form. Removal of the clitoris and part or all of the labia minora (the inner vaginal lips).

Type III (Infibulation): Removal of the external genitalia and stitching of the vaginal opening. A very small opening is left, about the diameter of a pencil. Sometimes the girl's or woman's legs are bound together from the hip to the ankle so that she cannot move for 40 days. Some communities don't stitch the opening. About 15 percent of women who undergo FGM have this form. In the areas where it is practiced, however, it sometimes affects 90 to 100 percent of the women.

Type IV: This category includes pricking, piercing or incision of the clitoris and/or labia, stretching the clitoris and/or labia, cauterization by burning of the clitoris and surrounding tissues, scraping (angurya cuts) of the vaginal orifice or cutting (gishiri cuts) of the vagina, introduction of corrosive substances into the vagina to cause bleeding, or introduction of herbs into the vagina to tighten or narrow the vagina, or any other procedure that falls under the definition of female genital mutilation.

The procedure is usually done outside of a hospital, with no anesthetic. The person (usually another woman) performing the procedure uses razors, scissors or knives, sometimes other sharp instruments. There are incidences of FGM being performed in hospitals as well. It is done to girls and women, the most common being girls under the age of puberty. . . .

Where Is It Being Done?

UNICEF [United Nations Children's Fund] estimates that the total number of women living today who have been subjected to FGM in Africa ranges between 100 and 130 million. This means that approximately 2 million girls are mutilated every year. Egypt, Ethiopia, Kenya, Nigeria, Somalia, and the Sudan account for 75 percent of all cases. In Djibouti and Somalia, 98 percent of girls are mutilated. Due to emigration, FGM is now being practiced in areas of Asia, Europe, and the United States.

The United Nations has declared that FGM is a violation of the human rights of girls and women.

Physical and Social Harm

FGM leads to lifelong pain and problems with sexual health and childbirth. Depending on the environment and type of the procedure, FGM can lead to serious health issues such as infection, illness and death. As a result, bleeding is severe, and infection can affect all or part of the genitals or reproductive organs. Due to infection, some women will find movement, sitting, urination and childbirth to be excruciatingly painful. Some women acquire dysmenorrhoea, which means they are no longer able to have periods. Fistula is another result of FGM, and is described as the continuous leakage of feces and urine, which can cause the woman to be outcast from her community.

Some women who have FGM performed on their daughters (or themselves) feel that they will be ostracized if they do not have the procedure done. Some women who have not undergone FGM feel pressured that they may not be able to find a husband. Men in communities that practice FGM add to the situation by asserting that a woman who is not cut is not fit to marry. Some men believe that FGM is the only way to prove a woman's virginity. These men think that if a woman is still sown together then she is a virgin. In addition, the act of opening her wounds for the act of sexual intercourse can be just as painful for the woman as the original procedure. The pressure to be accepted by their communities is the main reason women undergo FGM. While FGM is usually looked at as a cultural tradition, it is not required in any religion. It crosses ethnic, religious and cultural lines.

What Is Being Done to Stop It?

The United Nations has declared that FGM is a violation of the human rights of girls and women. The United States is calling for the complete elimination of FGM through policies that include education, the empowerment of women, and enforcement of laws against FGM. The performance of FGM on a person under the age of 18 was made a crime in the United States under section 116 of the Illegal Immigration Reform and Immigrant Responsibility Act of 1996, and 16 states have laws outlawing FGM.

Most countries where FGM is commonly performed do not have laws that prohibit FGM. If they do have such laws, the enforcement is often weak. There are a number of countries where immigrants are performing FGM, such as Sweden, the United Kingdom, Norway, Australia and New Zealand. Those countries have passed laws that outlaw the practice of FGM.

Due to the aspect of FGM as a cultural tradition, some organizations such as Amnesty International want to replace physical FGM with symbolic ceremonies. Instead of ignoring the strong cultural ties to the procedure and eliminating the part of FGM that is used as a rite of passage, Amnesty and other groups are advocating the redefining of the "rites in a way that promotes positive traditional values while removing the danger of physical and psychological harm."

Female Victims of Violence Face Obstacles Obtaining Asylum

Maria Bexelius

Maria Bexelius is the author of the book Women Refugees: An Analysis of Swedish Asylum Policy 1997–2000 *and was project coordinator for a one-year project (2002–2003) focusing on the rights of women asylum seekers in Sweden.*

Every night was the same. He forced her to have sex. If she offered the slightest resistance, he would cover her mouth, press her against her pillow and beat her while he was raping her. He would whisper "whore". He beat her during the day too. It happened when she disagreed with him, when she wore the "wrong" dress or did anything else that he didn't like. He would push her around, beat her and pull her hair. Sometimes he would whip her with a belt or burn her with cigarettes or with an iron. He used to keep her locked up. The beatings, rapes and constant death threats went on for years. In spite of her fears, she tried to report him to police, but it was in vain. Finally, she managed to flee him and her country.

Many of the tens of millions of people who have been displaced from their homes are women fleeing oppressive norms and violence. Some are women who may have opposed their oppression and stood up to the state, society, their husband or their relatives. Some are women whose only "wrongful" act was to have sex outside marriage or who have been raped. Some are women who have insisted on their right to choose for themselves which man or woman to love. Some are women who, consciously or unconsciously, through their actions or

Maria Bexelius, "Asylum-Seeking Women Confronted with Specific Obstacles," *Amnesty International, news.amnesty.org*, March 10, 2004. Reproduced by permission.

words, have transgressed social mores and therefore fear punishment from the state, from their communities or their families.

When Women Lack State Protection

International law is clear. Different forms of violence against women or other gender-related abuse constitute serious human rights abuses. In many cases, the violence constitutes torture or ill-treatment. These abuses are interlinked with one another as well as with the discrimination that stops women being treated as equal to men.

Historically, states have . . . been denying women equal access to protection in cases where they fear different forms of gender-related abuse.

At the very least, states have an obligation to protect women against violence and other gender-related abuse. It doesn't matter who the perpetrator may be or where the abuse takes place. But what if the state in one's homeland fails in its obligations to protect? What if a woman is forced to flee her country to escape abuse? Will she be able to find protection?

In order to ensure protection when a state fails to meet with its human rights obligations, the 1951 Convention relating to the Status of Refugees (the Refugee Convention) was adopted. It includes an agreed basis to decide who is a refugee deserving of international protection. According to the Convention, a refugee is any person who:

owing to well-founded fear of being persecuted for reasons of race, religion, nationality, membership of a particular social group or political opinion, is outside the country of [their] nationality and is unable or, owing to such fear, is unwilling to avail himself of the protection of that country; or who, not having a nationality and being outside the country of [their] former habitual residence, is unable or, owing to such fear, is unwilling to return to it.

Growing Awareness of Female Persecution

Although states have voluntarily taken on human rights obligations through signing the Refugee Convention, whether or not an individual refugee can assert her rights depends on how states choose to interpret it. Historically, states have applied a male-oriented interpretation based on men's experiences of persecution and they have, in that way, been denying women equal access to protection in cases where they fear different forms of gender-related abuse. This narrow interpretation may be traced back to 1951 when the Convention was drafted.

The problems women face can and must be solved. States must immediately make sure laws and practices are gender-sensitized.

However, over the decades, the international community has reacted to this neglect. In order to avoid the situation where men's experiences of persecution are the only model upon which asylum procedures would be based, the United Nations High Commissioner for Refugees (UNHCR) and other advocates working for women's and refugees' rights have repeatedly encouraged states to make necessary changes in the legislation and practice to ensure that women too get the protection they deserve. Gender guidelines have been introduced in several countries like Canada, the US and the UK that aim to end practices that discriminate against women.

Despite these positive steps, many asylum-seeking women are still confronted with obstacles from the day they arrive in the country in which they have sought refuge. Whenever this happens, in practical terms, an alliance has been forged between the country of asylum and the persecutors and authorities that can't or won't protect the women in the country of origin.

Obstacles for Asylum-Seeking Women

Sarah applied for asylum. She told her story to a decision-maker with the immigration authorities. But they denied her protection. They didn't consider her to be credible. One of their reasons was that she couldn't produce a doctor's certificate to prove that she had been beaten by her husband. Sarah appealed the decision, but was rejected again. The appeal authorities argued that the authorities in her home country would be able to provide her with protection against her husband in the case that she really felt threatened. Her fears of social ostracism and being forced into prostitution were not considered at all.

Many asylum-seeking women who flee violent abuse are not considered credible and, because of that, their claims for protection are rejected. Their credibility may be questioned when they do not give their interviewers an immediate, detailed and coherent briefing of their experiences of persecution, including of the sexual and physical abuse they may have suffered. The fact that victims of torture often fail to recollect the course of events chronologically and without contradictions is ignored.

Likewise, the fact that many sexually traumatised women have difficulties talking about the abuses because they feel dirty or ashamed (sometimes to the extent that they blame themselves), is also not being considered. The intimidation many feel when revealing intimate facts to officials, especially when the interviewer, interpreter and/or legal representative is a man, doesn't carry much weight either. Even those who do speak about their experiences face credibility problems, especially if there is insufficient documentary evidence (such as court documents, doctor's certificates and police reports) to support their claims, despite the fact that, for many women in many cases, these documents are extremely hard to come by.

Others are denied protection because there is no specific information about their country of origin to substantiate their claim. Sometimes the police or judicial authorities in the country of origin are expected to be able to offer adequate protection. This even happens in cases where women have already exhausted the possibilities open to them or have reason to disbelieve the willingness or ability of the authorities to offer protection. The fact that there are many examples of cases where women have been battered or killed after having filed reports with the police is disregarded.

Even when the facts are not contested, asylum-seeking women are still faced with states interpreting the Refugee Convention protection grounds from a male perspective. By doing that, they are not recognizing that women's political activities may be different from men's. Women who express their opinion about, for instance, gender-roles, or who act in a non-conforming way, may be transgressing the social mores and may risk punishment by state or non-state agents because of their actual or imputed political opinion.

To live a life free from violence is never an exaggerated claim; it is a fundamental human right.

Improving the Asylum Process for Women

The problems women face can and must be solved. States must immediately make sure laws and practices are gender-sensitized. This would mean that women asylum-seekers should always be interviewed separately by officials with thorough knowledge of the problems surrounding different forms of violence against women and other gender-related abuse. They must take into account the fact that women's experiences of persecution, as well as their own political activities, may be different from those of men and therefore demand that different questions are asked. Women interpreters, decision-makers and legal counsel with this competency must be available.

States must clarify that violence against women and serious discrimination based on gender are serious human rights abuses and should be covered by the concept of persecution. Determinations on whether an asylum-seeker's fear of persecution is well-founded, as well as the ability and willingness of a state to provide protection, must be made in the light of the personal experiences of the woman and thorough and accurate information about the status of women in the state, in society and in the family.

The lack of documentary evidence should not be decisive—guidance can be had from the principle of benefit of the doubt in favour of the applicant. It is also vital to look into questions on whether or not it is reasonable for a woman to try to actively seek the protection of the state or whether it is reasonable for her to find protection somewhere else in the country. Whether or not women's rights are upheld in the administration of justice as well as questions concerning age, class, caste, ethnicity and other status must be taken into account.

Concepts in the refugee definition such as *political opinion, religion* and *membership of a particular social group* must be interpreted in a way that ensure that women's protection needs are taken fully into account. Whenever someone applies for asylum on the basis of gender-related persecution, the principles on universality and equality and every individual's right to be free from violence are being tested.

Women worldwide have strategies to tackle violence and oppression and are engaging in acts of resistance when they demand respect and international protection from gender-related human rights abuses. In order to defend the universality of human rights and show solidarity with and respect for the individual woman, states have to uphold that right to international protection. To live a life free from violence is never an exaggerated claim; it is a fundamental human right.

If she is returned to her country of origin, Sarah fears that her husband will kill her or that she again will suffer beatings, rapes and constant death threats. She has no confidence in the willingness or ability of the police and other authorities to provide her with protection. Her family has disowned her. They consider her to be an unfit woman and wife for leaving her husband. She does not believe that she would be safe living on her own, and fears social ostracism and being forced into prostitution. She would rather kill herself. Psychologically she is suffering, and she is plagued by headaches. She has nightmares about the abuse, and every time she sees something or someone reminding her of her husband or the violence she has suffered, she is reliving it.

Organizations to Contact

The editors have compiled the following list of organizations concerned with the issues debated in this book. The descriptions are derived from materials provided by the organizations. All have publications or information available for interested readers. The list was compiled on the date of publication of the present volume; names, addresses, phone and fax numbers, and e-mail and Web site addresses may change. Be aware that many organizations take several weeks or longer to respond to inquiries, so allow as much time as possible.

American Bar Association Commission on Domestic Violence
740 Fifteenth Street NW, Washington, DC 20005
(202) 662-1000
e-mail: abacdv@abanet.org
Web site: www.abanet.org/domviol/home.html

The American Bar Association Commission on Domestic Violence researches model domestic violence programs in an effort to develop a blueprint for a national multidisciplinary domestic violence program. The commission provides information on domestic violence law and published several books, including *Stopping Violence Against Women: Using New Federal Laws* and *The Impact of Domestic Violence on Your Legal Practice: A Lawyer's Handbook*.

Battered Women's Support Services (BWSS)
PO Box 21503, 1424 Commercial Drive
Vancouver BC V5L 5G2
(604) 687-1868 • fax: (604) 687-1864
e-mail: information@bwss.org
Web site: www.bwss.org

Battered Women's Support Services (BWSS) provides education, advocacy, and support services to assist all battered women in Vancouver. BWSS works from a feminist perspective and seeks the elimination of all abuse of women. The organization publishes several service guides, educational pamphlets, and fliers.

Concerned Women for America (CWA)
1015 Fifteenth Street NW, Suite 1100, Washington, DC   20005
(202) 488-7000
Web site: www.cwfa.org

Concerned Women for America (CWA) seeks to protect the interests of American families, promote biblical values, and provide a voice for women throughout the United States who believe in Judeo-Christian values. CWA believes pornography contributes to abusive behavior in men. The organization publishes the bimonthly magazine *Family Voice*.

Faith Trust Institute
2400 North Forty-fifth Street, #10, Seattle, WA   98103
(206) 634-1903 • fax: (206) 634-0115
e-mail: info@faithtrustinstitute.org
Web site: www.faithtrustinstitute.org

The Faith Trust Institute is an interreligious ministry addressing issues of sexual and domestic violence. Its goal is to engage religious leaders in the task of ending abuse through institutional and social change. The institute publishes educational videos, the quarterly *Journal of Religion and Abuse*, and numerous books including *Violence Against Women and Children: A Christian Theological Sourcebook* and *Sexual Violence: The Unmentionable Sin—an Ethical and Pastoral Perspective*.

Family Research Laboratory (FRL)
University of New Hampshire, Durham, NH   03824
(603) 862-1888
Web site: www.unh.edu/frl

Family Research Laboratory (FRL) is an independent research unit devoted to the study of the causes and consequences of family violence, and it also works to dispel myths about family violence through public education. It publishes numerous books and articles on violence between men and women, marital rape, and verbal aggression. FRL's Web site offers a complete list of available materials, such as the article "Stress and Rape in the Context of American Society," and the book *Understanding Partner Violence: Prevalence, Causes, Consequences, and Solutions.* However, many of the publications are intended for research scholars rather than the general public.

The Fatherhood Coalition (CPF)
PO Box 700, Milford, MA 01757
(617) 723-DADS
Web site: www.fatherhoodcoalition.org

The Fatherhood Coalition (CPF) is an organization of men and women advocating the institution of fatherhood. The coalition works to promote shared parenting and to end the discrimination and persecution faced by divorced and unwed fathers, in society at large and specifically in Massachusetts. CPF is active in the fight against the abuse of restraining orders, especially in divorce cases. The organization's Web site offers articles and links to other pro-fatherhood and male advocacy groups.

Feminist Majority Foundation
The National Center for Women & Policing
Beverly Hills, CA 90212
(310) 556-2526 • fax: (310) 556-2509
e-mail: womencops@feminist.org
Web site: www.womenandpolicing.org

The Feminist Majority Foundation is an activist organization that works to eliminate sex discrimination and social and economic injustice. Its National Center for Women & Policing believes that female police officers respond more effectively to incidents of violence against women than do their male counterparts. It acts as a nationwide resource for law enforcement agencies and community leaders seeking to increase the number of female police officers in their communities and to improve police response to family violence. Its publications include *The Annual Survey on the Status of Women in Policing*, the *Study on the Gender Gap in Use of Force*, and the quarterly *Feminist Majority Report*.

Independent Women's Forum

1726 M Street NW, Tenth Floor, Washington, DC 20036
(202) 419-1820
e-mail: info@iwf.org
Web site: www.iwf.org

The Independent Women's Forum is a conservative women's advocacy group that believes in individual freedom and personal responsibility and promotes common sense over feminism. The forum believes that the incidence of domestic violence is exaggerated and that the Violence Against Women Act is ineffective and unjust. The Web site features numerous articles and a daily blog called Ink Well.

National Clearinghouse on Marital and Date Rape

2325 Oak Street, Berkeley, CA 94708
Web site: www.members.aol.com/ncmdr/index.html

The National Clearinghouse on Marital and Date Rape operates as a consulting firm on issues of marital, cohabitant, and date rape. It attempts to educate the public and to establish social and political equality in intimate relationships. Its publications include *Marital Rape Victims Fight Back, Prosecution Statistics on Marital Rape*, and the pamphlet *State Law Chart on Marital Rape.*

National Coalition Against Domestic Violence (NCADV)

1120 Lincoln Street, Suite 1603, Denver, CO 80203
(303) 839-1852 • fax: 303-831-9251
Web site: www.ncadv.org

The National Coalition Against Domestic Violence (NCADV) is dedicated to the empowerment of battered women and is committed to the elimination of personal and societal violence in the lives of battered women and their children. The organization's work includes coalition building at the local, state, regional, and national levels; support for the provision of community-based, nonviolent alternatives—such as safe home and shelter programs—for battered women and their children; public education and technical assistance; policy development and innovative legislation; focus on the leadership of NCADV's caucuses and task forces developed to represent the concerns of organizationally underrepresented groups; and efforts to eradicate social conditions that contribute to violence against women and children. Publications include *General Information Packet: Every Home a Safe Home* and the *National Directory of Domestic Violence Programs: A Guide to Community Shelter, Safe Homes, and Service Programs.*

National Coalition of Anti-Violence Programs
240 West Thirty-fifth Street, Suite 200, New York, NY   10001
(212) 714-1184 • fax: (212) 714-2627
e-mail: info@ncavp.org
Web site: www.ncavp.org

The National Coalition of Anti-Violence Programs serves lesbian, gay, transgender, bisexual, and HIV-positive victims of violence, and others affected by violence, by providing free and confidential services enabling them to regain their sense of control, identify and evaluate their options, and assert their rights. By educating law enforcement and social service agency personnel and calling attention to inadequate official and professional responses, the organization works to hold law enforcement and social service agencies accountable to their obligation for impartial service. The organization also tracks and publishes statistical reports of hate crimes and domestic violence. All reports and media releases are available on its Web site.

National Criminal Justice Reference Service (NCJRS)
PO Box 6000, Rockville, MD   20849
(800) 851-3420 • fax: (301) 519-5212

e-mail: askncjrs@ncjrs.org
Web site: www.ncjrs.gov

A component of the Office of Justice Programs of the U.S. Department of Justice, the National Criminal Justice Reference Service (NCJRS) supports and conducts research on crime, criminal behavior, and crime prevention. It also acts as a clearinghouse for criminal justice information. Many reports are available from the NCJRS, including *Domestic Violence, Stalking, and Antistalking, Acquaintance Rape of College Students*, and *Civil Protection Orders: Victims' Views on Effectiveness*.

**The National Organization for Men
Against Sexism (NOMAS)**
PO Box 455, Louisville, CO   80027
(303) 666-7043
e-mail: info@nomas.org
Web site: www.nomas.org

The National Organization for Men Against Sexism (NOMAS) is an activist organization of men and women supporting positive changes for men. NOMAS advocates a perspective for enhancing men's lives that is pro-feminist, gay affirmative, antiracist, and committed to justice on a broad range of social issues, including class, age, religion, and physical abilities. The organization publishes a quarterly journal called *Brother*, as well as occasional position papers and briefs such as "Manhood and Violence: The Deadliest Equation." All publications are available on the Web site.

The Network/La Red
PO Box 6011, Boston, MA   02114
(617) 695-0877 • fax: (617) 423-5651
e-mail: info@thenetworklared.org
Web site: www.thenetworklared.org

The Network/La Red has become a national resource and model to end abuse in lesbian, bisexual women's, and transgender communities. Through community education and outreach, its members encourage communities to recognize and eliminate battering, homophobia, and misogyny. The Network/La Red provides free and confidential advocacy for victims, information about intimate abuse, and a reading list of sources addressing lesbian, bisexual, and transgender violence.

U.S. Department of Justice Office on Violence Against Women
800 K Street NW, Suite 920, Washington, DC 20530
(202) 307-6026 • fax: (202) 307-3911
Web site: www.usdoj.gov/ovw

The U.S. Department of Justice Office on Violence Against Women is responsible for the overall coordination and focus of Department of Justice efforts to combat violence against women. It maintains the National Domestic Violence Hotline and publishes a monthly newsletter. An online domestic violence awareness manual is available on the Web site along with press releases, speeches, and the full text of and news about the Violence Against Women Act.

Women's Freedom Network (WFN)
4410 Massachusetts Avenue NW, Suite 179
Washington, DC 20016
(202) 885-6245
e-mail: wfn@american.edu
Web site: www.womensfreedom.org

The Women's Freedom Network (WFN) was founded in 1993 by a group of women who were seeking alternatives to both extremist ideological feminism and antifeminism traditionalism. It opposes gender bias in the sentencing of spouse abusers and believes acts of violence against women should be considered individually rather than stereotyped as gender-based hate crimes. WFN publishes a newsletter and books including *Neither Victim nor Enemy: Women's Freedom Network Looks at Gender in America.*

Bibliography

Books

Joanne Belknap   *The Invisible Woman: Gender, Crime, and Justice.* Belmont, CA: Wadsworth Publishing, 2007.

Sandra L. Brown   *Family Interventions in Domestic Violence: A Handbook of Gender-Inclusive Theory and Treatment.* New York: Springer, 2007.

Shamita Das Dasgupta, ed.   *Body Evidence: Intimate Violence Against South Asian Women in America.* New Brunswick, NJ: Rutgers University Press, 2007.

Michael Domitrz   *Voices of Courage: Inspiration from Survivors of Sexual Assault.* Greenfield, WI: Awareness Publications, 2005.

Donald Dutton   *The Abusive Personality: Violence and Control in Intimate Relationships.* New York: Guilford Press, 2007.

Elizabeth Kandel Englander   *Understanding Violence.* Mahwah, NJ: Lawrence Erlbaum, 2007.

Diane Glass   *Stalking the Stalker: Fighting Back with High-Tech Gadgets and Low-Tech Know-How.* New York: iUniverse, 2006.

| Karen Heimer and Candace Krut, eds. | *Gender and Crime: Patterns of Victimization and Offending.* New York: New York University Press, 2006. |

| Marianne Hester, Chris Pearson, Nicola Harwin, and Hilary Abrahams | *Making an Impact: Children and Domestic Violence: A Reader.* Philadelphia: J. Kingsley, 2007. |

| Richard T. Hise | *The War Against Men.* Oakland, OR: Elderberry Press, 2004. |

| Christina Hoff | *The War Against Boys: How Misguided Feminism Is Harming Our Young Men.* New York: Simon & Schuster, 2004. |

| Nicky Ali Jackson, ed. | *Encyclopedia of Domestic Violence.* New York: Routledge, 2007. |

| Ellyn Kaschak, ed. | *Intimate Betrayal: Domestic Violence in Lesbian Relationships.* Binghamton, NY: Haworth Press, 2002. |

| George B. Kehner | *Date Rape Drugs.* New York: Chelsea House, 2004. |

| Eileen Regan Larence | *Prevalence of Domestic Violence, Sexual Assault, Dating Violence, and Stalking.* Washington, DC: U.S. Government Accountability Office, 2006. |

| Catharine A. MacKinnon | *Women's Lives, Men's Laws.* Cambridge, MA: Belknap Press, 2005. |

| Lesley McMillan | *Feminists Organising Against Gendered Violence.* London: Palgrave, 2007. |

Periodicals

Marc Angelucci and Glenn Sacks	"California Domestic Violence Lawsuit Will Help Secure Services for All Abuse Victims," *Los Angeles Daily Journal*, May 16, 2007.
Emily Bazar	"Stalking 'Definitely a Problem' for Women at College," *USA Today*, April 4, 2007.
Emily Cadei	"Abused to Death: An Epidemic of 'Intimate Femicide' in South Africa," *Ms.*, Fall 2006.
Jane Chestnut	"Linda Fairstein," *Woman's Day*, February 1, 2007.
Judy Dutton	"When Girls Bully Girls," *Biography*, January 2003.
Steven Erlanger	"Violence Against Palestinian Women Is Increasing, Study Says," *New York Times*, November 7, 2006.
Bay Fang	"The Talibanization of Iraq," *Ms.*, Spring 2007.
Bob Herbert	"Punished for Being Female," *New York Times*, November 2, 2006.
Bose Ironsi	"The Bleeding That Never Stops: The Situation of Women's Human Rights in Nigeria," *Women's World*, 2007.
Miranda Kennedy	"Cheaper than a Cow: Trapped in India's Poverty, a Family Sells a Daughter into Sexual Servitude," *Ms.*, Spring 2004.

Jeffrey Kluger   "Taming Wild Girls," *Time*, April 24, 2006.

Alfred   "Darfur Refugees Plead for U.N.
de Montesquiou   Help," *Time*, April 24, 2007.

Karen Morgaine   "Domestic Violence and Human Rights: Local Challenges to a Universal Framework," *Journal of Sociology & Social Welfare*, March 2007.

Sara Nordstrom   "16 Days of Activism Against Gender Violence," *Gender and Development*, November 2006.

Peta Owens-   "Where Mother's Day Strikes Thrice,"
Liston   *Time*, May 11, 2007.

Katha Pollitt   "'Democracy' Is Hell," *Nation*, May 28, 2007.

Julieanne Porter   "Resources," *Gender and Development*, March 2007.

Anna Quindlen   "Frightening—And Fantastic," *Newsweek*, September 18, 2006.

Julie Scelfo and   "Bad Girls Go Wild," *Newsweek*, June
William Lee   13, 2005.
Adams

Wairagala Wakabi   "Africa Battles to Make Female Genital Mutilation History," *Lancet*, March 31, 2007.

Internet Source

Courtney E. Martin	"Willful Ignorance," *American Prospect*, January 17, 2007. www.prospect.org/cs/articles?article=willful_ignorance.

Index